A Nation of Sheep

WILLIAM J. LEDERER

A
Nation of
Sheep

W · W · NORTON & COMPANY · INC · *New York*

Contents

Acknowledgments

WITHOUT the help, direct and indirect, of many people this book could not have been written. My thanks to the late Dr. Thomas A. Dooley, Professor Claude Buss, Professor John King Fairbank, Professor Mason Hammond, Dr. Edward W. Wagner, Professor Eugene Burdick, Professor Philip Selznick, Professor Arthur M. Schlesinger, Sr., Barbara Rex, Avis De Voto, Ella Emery, Harriet Joesting, Louis Lyons, Mark Mancall, Charles Bernard, Professor John Stalker, Wayne Collins, John Reddan, Frank Valeo, Cal Scollin, George Chaplin, Dorothy Moore, Ethel Lederer, Brian Lederer, Albert and Marjorie Ravenholt, Doctor Willard Hanna, Doctor Dwight Dill, Sigma Delta Chi, Ambassador John Allison, William Mullahey, William Stucky, Sam Frankel, Pickett Lumpkin, and John Lacy. My special thanks to Eric Swenson, without whose patient editing the book never would have been completed; and to Elliott Perkins of Lowell House, Harvard University, whose thoughtfulness and hospitality gave me an effective place to work; and to the students of Lowell House, whose good company provided stimulus and encouragement. My thanks also to a score of other good friends whose names I, ingrate, have neglected to note. Naturally some of the above may disagree with my views; and of course, if there are any errors they are my own.

William J. Lederer

Preface

IN THE two and a half years since *The Ugly American* was published, more than 8,000 readers have written Eugene Burdick and myself. Letters have come from every corner of the country and from all kinds of people in every conceivable occupation. By and large, however, they have been from "ordinary" citizens and they have, in one form or another, asked the same questions: what can the average citizen do about the posture of the United States in foreign affairs? How can the man in the street help prevent the blunders by which we have aided our enemies to turn against us in large areas of the world—areas where our influence was paramount and admiration for us high, fifteen short years ago.

These are disturbing questions, and certainly Professor Burdick and I gave no more than hints as to their solutions in *The Ugly American*. The key to the riddle lies in the causes of the blunders; and the chief cause is ignorance—an overwhelming national ignorance of the facts about the rest of the world. A nation, or an individual, cannot function unless the truth is available and understood. Since the United States is a democracy, the broad answer to the questions asked in the 8,000 *Ugly American* letters is that all of us must become informed.

Like most simple solutions, it is a difficult one to apply. Particularly it is difficult in the United States today, when the truth is largely unavailable; when the government itself frequently is ignorant of the most obvious events occurring in other nations; when the press is so convinced that the American people don't want the hard facts of foreign affairs that it makes only routine efforts to report them; when lack of knowledge of international matters has made of the people of the United States a nation of sheep—uneasy, but too apathetic and uninformed to know why—endorsing any solutions which appear cheap and easy and which come from a source apparently better informed than themselves.

This book has been written in the conviction that something can be done about it, and that it must be the average citizen who does it. It is, I hope, a useful answer to the questions implied in *The Ugly American*.

W. J. Lederer
Lowell House
Cambridge, Massachusetts

10 December 1960

I
Some Stories

1

The Laos Fraud

THE DESTRUCTION of a mighty nation may well be approaching because of the activities of one person. He has encouraged leaders to tranquilize the populace with half-truths. He has lured the press into inattention and has assisted the people in duping themselves. He has persuaded his fellow citizens to concentrate on life's comic strips and mindless entertainments and to avoid the bruises of reality.

The culprit is the person whose eyes scan these words, and whose hands—at this moment—hold this book. The country is the United States of America.

A companion in guilt is the author who, for many years, failed as a patriot. Like most average Americans, he accepted the privileges of citizenship but rejected its responsibilities.

The results are tragic. Today we are a nation of fair-weather citizens who serve their country only if they receive financial security and vast luxuries, of sloths who try to bribe neutral nations into cooperation. We are a nation of people who are afraid to speak up on unpopular issues and who clamor for leisure time without knowing how to use it, whose self-indulgence has blinded us to the real dangers of our time.

The defeat of America need not be accomplished by destructive weapons and violence. There are easier and cheaper ways of conquering a politically incompetent nation. It can be accomplished by psychological weapons, by economic strangulation, by political chicanery, by intellectual subversion.

Such a finale need never occur; it cannot occur to an informed, intelligent people. But today we are adrift in a sea of misinformation; and what happens when ignorance is in control is indicated by recent events in the tiny nation of Laos. What many Americans accepted as a blurred, passing vignette of history is, in hard fact, a bitter warning. The episode in Laos is an omen with the most frightening of implications.

In the summer of 1959 there occurred a series of events which demonstrated our national ignorance in a shameful and nearly fatal manner. Briefly, the United States threatened intervention in a foreign country for reasons which, it turned out, had no basis in fact. The people of the United States were led to believe that Laos physically had been invaded by foreign Communist troops from across its northern border. Our Secretary of State called the situation grave; our ambassador to the U.N. called for world action; our press carried scare headlines; our senior naval officer implied armed intervention and was seconded by ranking Congressmen, including the Chairman of the National Committee of the Republican Party, which was then in power.

The entire affair was a fraud. No military invasion of Laos had taken place. Yet for weeks, neither our government nor our press bothered to investigate at first hand. As a result, we came close to triggering war, on false information not of our own gathering. We did in fact make fools of ourselves in the eyes of our friends and "imperialist warmongers" of ourselves in the words of our enemies and in the opinion of neutrals.

The case of Laos is not an isolated one; alas, it is typical. It is worth exploring in detail for what it shows about a nation uninformed.

Laos is a small nation—about the size of Idaho or Yugoslavia—and is mostly swamps, jungles, and mountains. There are only 700 telephones. Population figures are nonexistent, although anthropologists believe there are about 1,500,000 inhabitants, most of whom suffer from disease. The people are scattered about in tiny, isolated villages. A large proportion of the Laos don't know the name of their king; or of the nation of which they are citizens.

Ninety-five percent of them have never seen or heard a radio. With the exception of several big towns, there is no electricity. Roads are almost non-existent. Newspapers are unknown. The only way people can get information is when someone comes to their village and tells them in their own dialect.

The Lao government, which we have been supporting since 1955, has done almost nothing to improve the country's health, or to alleviate its poverty and ignorance. Citizens are so distrustful of their officials that when tax collectors or a platoon of the Royal Lao Army comes to a village, the entire population usually takes to the hills.

Laos, therefore, is perfectly tailored for subversion. But why should anyone wish to subvert a little country which appears to be low-grade real estate?

True, Laos itself is, at present, not a rich land. But strategically and politically it appears to be the key to a treasure chest, a magic chunk of territory which borders six important Asian nations. Laos is a corridor, an access point, to Thailand, South Vietnam, Malaya, Burma, and Cambodia. It is the northern point of a natural highway which the Chinese Communists hope to follow as far south as Indonesia.

Laos may well be the foothold by which Red China can open the door to Southeast Asia's rice bowl, vast oil reserves, and untapped mineral deposits—as well as a supply of labor which is greater than the population of the United States. If Red China should acquire this rich peninsula which is just south of Laos, she would also get a strategic position flanking Australia, New Zealand, and India. It would allow her to snuff out Japan's Southeast Asia trade, without which Japan could be forced to join the Communist axis.

This, then, is why little Laos—a land of swamps, jungles, mountains and illiterate, sick people—is so important. This is why—even though Laos is isolated, politically fragmented, distant, and mysterious—we must know what goes on there.

North Vietnamese-trained Communists have made it their business to become experts on Laos. Taking advantage of the guerrilla warfare which has long been flickering between the northern and southern tribes, trained Red organizers went to work in the Laotian swamps and jungles, propagandizing the individual Lao on a daily face-to-face basis. Who are these Communists? It is difficult to identify them. Many are tribesmen who have been living in Laos for generations—for example the Khas (Captain Kong Le who led the coup d'état in August of 1960 is a Kha). Some are more recent arrivals; and some tribesmen belong half to Laos, half to North Vietnam. The borders are not marked.

The Reds agitated and goaded an already restless people into further dissent against the Royal Lao government. The villagers bitterly resented "any meddling by officials of the rich boys in Vientiane" in their local affairs. By 1955 it was clear that the Communists might split Laos into two nations. Or worse yet, the Royal family might swing entirely over to the Communists as a means of survival.

Laos continued drifting towards anti-Americanism, and a harried U. S. State Department, unable and apparently unwilling to communicate directly with the Lao people, continued desperately to seek a magic, immediate solution. Diplomatic bribery is a crude way of describing the American method; but it is a realistic explanation of the Department of State decision to pour vast fortunes into tiny Laos. The first installment was to be about $35 million, most of it earmarked for the Laotian army of 25,000 men.

· 15 ·

It was hoped that by this method (in some miraculous, unplanned way), the $35,000,000 would find its way into circulation and improve the common man's standards of living and thereby stiffen his resistance to Communism.

How did the State Department decide that $35 million a year was required to stabilize Laos? A Congressional investigation revealed that no experts had been sent in to study the needs. No cost tests had been run. The U. S. Government's representatives simply went to the Laotian Minister of Defense and asked the price of operating a 25,000-man army.

The U. S. Department of Defense objected. There was no military reason for a 25,000-man army in Laos, according to the Joint Chiefs of Staff. But after a polite argument, the diplomats overruled the Pentagon. Political urgency demanded the dumping of money in Laos. And that was that. Apparently it was believed that there was no time to find out the facts for ourselves.

During the next five years about $235 millions were shipped to Laos, and approximately 75% of it went into an almost make-believe Laotian army. The greatest portion of the money was handed over in cash; and much of it mysteriously disappeared from public view.

Laotian officials refused to tell American administrators what happened to the money; and they refused to let anyone examine the books. In fact, in many cases there were no books. U. S. diplomats, unwilling to offend Laotian officials, swallowed their pride and said nothing. The fear of offending was strange, especially as Laos *was receiving more aid per capita than any country in the world*. The price of maintaining one Lao soldier was approximately twice as much as that of any other allied nation receiving U. S. military aid.

During the next five years of American assistance to Laos, the ruling clique had a gay time. For example, before the aid started, there had only been about 300 automobiles in Vientiane, the capital. A quarter of a billion dollars of aid later, the muddy streets were crowded with thousands of luxury cars. Vientiane, which previously had been a dull and austere town with hardly one decent restaurant, now had nightclubs charging $2.00 for a drink. Entertainment came from pretty hostesses imported from Hongkong, Bangkok, Manila, and Saigon. Stores bulged with foreign commodities which the average Laotian neither could afford nor knew anything about. Some of the merchandise came from Red China.

The Seventh Report by the House of Representatives Committee on Government Operations indicates that a small number of Lao (who were close to the U. S. Embassy) had become enormously rich via black market, currency manipulation, and just plain palm-greasing. A few Americans also had dipped their itching fingers into the gravy bowl. One, a Mr. McNamara, presently is under indictment by Federal Grand Jury for accepting $13,500 in cumshaw. Another "got his" by selling his useless $400 cadillac to a contractor for several thousand dollars. The following day the contractor dumped it into a dry well. All of Vientiane saw it; and the American government was the laughing-stock of the country. Everyone in the rich capital seemed to be making money, but the common people of Laos, particularly the tribesmen in the interior and in the hills, got nothing; and they began to grumble. The poor man's bamboo telegraph slowly spread descriptions of the governmental corruption resulting from U. S. aid. These descriptions happened to conform perfectly with Communist propaganda; and the Laos' confidence in the Communists became stronger.

Despite the secrecy clamped around the Laos aid operation (not even Congress could get information), news of scandals, corruption, and inefficiency began to leak out to America. Articles appeared in publications such as *The Wall Street Journal, The Reader's Digest,* and *The New York Times.*

In the spring of 1958 the Congressional Sub-Committee on the Far East and the Pacific of the Committee on Foreign Affairs began investigating rumors of alarming waste, frauds, and ineffectiveness of the U. S. program in Laos. Then the Committee on Government Operations also started hearings. The major witnesses—U. S. officials who had supervised Laotian aid—denied that the wastes, frauds and inefficiency had been harmful to the total U. S. effort. Ambassador Parsons, who had been in charge during the most corrupt periods (later promoted to Assistant Secretary of State for Far Eastern Affairs), made a persuasive argument. His total testimony gave the unmistakable impression that even if the methods of the United States were not very efficient, how else could we get a job done in a hurry? An immediate emergency had to be met. Why all the hubbub? After all, the American objectives had been realized. The United States had been successful in beating the Communists in Laos. There had just been a Laotian national election, Mr. Parsons pointed out. Although the final results were not fully known, it was obvious that the Communists had suffered a bad defeat at the polls. The later Assistant Secretary of State Parsons said:

> We have no authoritative information from United States sources but we have been given information which is said to be official on the early results on the first 15 of the 21 seats at stake. If this information is confirmed, the Communist Pathet Laos will have won only 2 out of 15 seats . . . [there followed a detailed description of what this meant]. If this is the situation—and I hope I am not overconfident when I express some confident optimism—if this is the situation in Laos, it will be due, in part, to our aid and will, I hope, indicate, in part, what you gentlemen and the rest of us will have received in value for our aid money. It is not all, of course, that we will have done with that money, because we have brought aid of various kinds to the people of Laos but the main point is that the integrity and independence of Laos in the free world will have been preserved. It may be also that we will have arrived at a point where we can reduce the costs to the taxpayer in the future . . .

It would be difficult to conceive of finer results from a U. S. aid program. It was duly reported by the press of the nation.

A few days later the votes were counted. Contrary to the State Department's optimism based on sources "said to be official," *the Communists had won a sensational victory*. So sensational, in fact, that the pro-Red leader of the rebels had to be installed in the Royal Cabinet as the minister who controlled U. S. Foreign Aid funds to Laos. A further irony, two battalions of pro-Communist troops from now on would be supported by U. S. funds. We now would be buying the guns, food, and bullets for the soldiers who had been fighting the government we supported.

Where did the State Department get its false information? On what grounds could J. Graham Parsons, the ex-ambassador, reach such an optimistic and erroneous conclusion? Later he was promoted to a position in which he was responsible for the execution of U. S. policy in the entire Far East. How is it that no one knew enough about Laos to query him when his appointment was up for confirmation? These are important questions to ponder. We must assume, of course, that the U. S. Embassy in Laos had a staff of Asian experts who were supposed to know what was happening; and that the Central Intelligence Agency and U. S. military intelligence operators were willing and able to advise the ambassador. Therefore, when a policy-maker, officially representing the State Department, gives misleading information to the Congress, something of major magnitude is askew.

Congress rightfully became suspicious and continued investigating. With reasonableness and dignity, without publicity, witnesses were questioned, papers studied, and on-the-spot surveys made. A year later, on June 15, 1959, Congress published the results: *The Seventh Report by the Committee on Government Operations.*

The report was fifty-one pages of shocking disclosures on Laos. For example:

". . . in summary, the decision to support a 25,000 man army—motivated by a Department of State desire to provide political stability—seems to have been the foundation for a series of developments which *detract* from that stability.

"The aid program has not prevented the spread of Communism in Laos. In fact the Communist victory in last year's elections based on the slogans of 'Government corruption' and 'Government indifference' might lead one to conclude that the U. S. aid program had contributed to an atmosphere in which the ordinary people of Laos question the value of friendship of the United States."*

The Report on Laos also said, ". . . giving Laos more foreign aid than it could absorb, hindered rather than helped . . . excessive *cash* grants forced money into the Lao economy at a faster rate than it could possibly be absorbed, causing: . . . inflation . . . profiteering."

The implication was obvious. Congress had heard about too many failures, inefficiencies, corruptions, bribes, Cadillacs-in-wells, and useless "Peabody Parkways"; and the Congress was inclined to reduce funds to Laos. This was the last thing the Department of State or ICA (International Cooperation Administration) wanted. Most of all, the politicians and rich merchants of Laos didn't want the bonanza to end.

Now, the Big Deception began to go into action.

The question for the Laotian government, at this time, then, would be how to persuade the U. S. Congress and U. S. public that aid for Laos should not be reduced. What reasons could be offered for having an army which costs

* The Congressional Report, entitled: *U. S. Aid Operations in Laos,* Seventh Report by the Committee on Government Operations, on how American officials received bribes, how fact-finders were railroaded out of the country by the ambassador, of financial collusion and corruption, can be obtained by writing: Committee on Government Operations, House Office Building, Washington 25, D. C.

three times as much as the total cash income of Laos? Millions of U. S. dollars already had gone into the hodgepodge Laotian military, yet there was little to show for it. There was no checking-up on padded army payrolls; and much of the money went into officers' pockets. Only about one-fifth of the troops could be put into the field. They had no communications system, no transport system, no system of materiel maintenance, and precious few functional weapons, in spite of the enormous sums spent. The Royal Laotian troops were incapable of handling the pro-Reds—who were far fewer in number than themselves.

Naturally the Congress would be skeptical about appropriating further large sums. In the early summer of 1959 many members of Congress began to lose confidence in the Asian policies of the State Department and ICA. The Congress still recognized the need for a foreign-aid program, but was apprehensive over its shabby administration; especially as blunders and corruptions similar to those discovered in Laos were being brought to light in other countries.

What went through the heads of the Lao officials we can only guess. But of this we are certain: within a week after the damning Congressional Report was received in Laos, things began to happen. The government of Laos announced to the world—via American diplomatic channels and the American press—that their freedom-loving little nation suddenly was the victim of a vicious "invasion" from a foreign Communist aggressor. (The Communist broadcasts made the first announcement. This should have aroused American suspicions. But it did not.)

The headlines were dramatic.

New York World-Telegram

The Sun

SPORTS FINAL

VOL. 127—NO. 8 — NEW YORK, SATURDAY, SEPTEMBER 5, 1959 TEN CENTS

Herter Tackles Laos Crisis

Back in U.S., Calls

BOSTON SUNDAY HERALD

BOSTON, SUNDAY, SEPTEMBER 6, 1959—ONE HUNDRED SIXTY-EIGHT PAGES

★★★★

UN Security Council Called to Act Tomorrow

U.S. TO ASK OBSERVERS IN LA

Los Angeles Times

FINAL
ALL THE NEWS
ALL THE TIME

Hot

340 PAGES   21   SUNDAY 20

TUTION

Laos Troops Locked
n Battle With Reds

Laos' Royal City

USS BORDER
HARDS SHOOT
WN TURKS

Planes Fly In Supplies;
Outposts of Governmen
Reported in Enemy Han

ANKARA, Turkey.

VIENTIANE, Laos, Aug. 22 (UPI)—Royal Lao
troops were reported today to be locked in a
battle with communist forces in Northern Laos.
Reds were believed to have taken several
outposts.

Panics as Reds

At the same time, the communist press said that "peace

PEACE PLAN
466,000
393,000

Province

The Washington Post

Times Herald

SUNDAY, SEPTEMBER 6, 1959

HEAVY FIGH

U.S. Links War in Lao
Moscow and Peking

FLARE

And so Laos was "invaded." It was a widely reported invasion, dominating headlines, demanding and receiving statements from U. S. officials, and complete with frantically worded communiqués from the combat areas.

Stimulated by such inflammatory news, there was wild talk in Congress of sending U. S. troops to Laos, and of bombing the "invaders" with U. S. Navy and Air Force planes. Units of the Seventh Fleet were sent to the danger zone in the South China Sea. The President said he would like to talk to Mr. Khrushchev about the matter. State Department announced that the situation was grave. The press did its part:

> Admiral Arleigh A. Burke, Chief of Naval Operations, said today that the Navy "might" be called into the Laotian crisis.
> (August 10)

> Laotian Reds in Big Drive Using North Vietnamese Units. (a headline on September 2)

> The United States can send combat-ready fighters and fighter bombers to Laos in thirty-five hours, the head of the Tactical Air Command said today.
> (September 4)

> Senator Thruston B. Morton predicted here today that the West would furnish Laos with manpower as well as arms if such aid were required to halt Communist aggression.
> (September 22)

Tons of urgent defense materiel were frantically airlifted to Laos. Millions of dollars of extra funds were spent in assistance. Nobody said how much. The Laotians knew, the Reds probably knew; but the American people were kept in ignorance.

Even though we did not know the exact amount, we as a nation certainly approved the vigorous quasi-military action taken. We were convinced that a Red invasion was pouring over the Laotian borders. *Not subversion, but a great physical attack.* There seemed no doubt that a war embracing thousands of troops, tanks, planes, and mass battles, was raging. Regardless of how the accounts were worded, this was the picture given the nation.

It was understood that with all the apprehension the government was showing and the pessimistic attitude of the Congress, that the invasion and fighting in Laos must be an overwhelming battle; and that before the United States began to get ready for another hot war, our experts— as well as the public—surely knew all about the situation in Laos; and were familiar with exact details of the "invasion" from North Vietnam.

The truth is that *The U. S. government was in almost total ignorance of the facts. There was not a single American observer in the so-called combat area. There was not one official U. S. eye-witness to any of the "invasion" activities.*

The President of the United States, the Secretary of State, the Chairman of the Senate Foreign Relations Committee, our military leaders, and hundreds of professional journalists employed as headline writers excited the nation and demanded drastic action on a "foreign invasion" about which they had not one shred of first-hand information.

The near-hysteria which followed was based on briefings by Laotian officials. Or, to make things worse, it was often based on third-hand reports originating with Laos officials.

Here is what Dennis Warner, the great Australian war correspondent, reported from the Laotian town of Samneua. (Please note that Samneua was not active combat front—even though some American publications used this as a dateline, and implied that the correspondents cabling from there were in the thick of the battle.)

". . . Despite the Royal Lao government's official claims of invasions and major border crossings, Laos suffered far more from subversion than from armed aggression.

". . . But what had actually happened? There were co-ordinated attacks in the region of the North Vietnam border, certainly. But the stories brought back by refugees and escapees were highly exaggerated. I spoke to one Lao noncommissioned officer, with General Amkha himself acting as interpreter, and found that the general accepted as a fact what the most junior western staff officer would have rejected as fiction. Piecing together all the reports from his defeated soldiers and throwing in civilian alarmist reports for good measure, General Amkha believed that a total of 3,500 enemy troops were advancing on Samneua. But apart from sounding the knell of defeat, he did little else. A second examination of his war map showed that though four days had elapsed since the attack north of Samneua, he had made no attempt to send out patrols or to establish contact with the enemy. The war map was, in fact, based largely on refugee stories and rumor, and even on defeatist's tales spread deliberately by enemy agents."

It was this type of haphazard information—glibly handed out in foreign governmental communiqués—which twisted U. S. public opinion, and influenced the course of U. S. foreign policy.

There were over 200 U. S. professional military men in Vientiane; and approximately an equal number of U. S. civilians—supposed to be Asian experts—attached to the American Embassy's country team. But they failed to get into the alleged combat area to observe and report what was going on. They didn't even see or interview the Communist prisoners mentioned in official Laotian communiqués. There are indications that even these were fake.

The information the American civil servants passed on to their government and country was hearsay; but it was acted upon as though it were verified fact.

American journalists (and among them were some of the best in the profession) fared no better. It was not until the end of September, several months after the trouble started, that correspondents got to the northern provinces where the so-called war allegedly took place.

It was during those several months of rumors and headlines that the American press and government acted as loudspeakers for the propaganda relayed by Laotians. True, the accounts cabled by journalists usually said that the stories came from foreign sources. But Americans have sloppy news-reading habits. We accept the headline's scream as the full story and miss the fine (but important) points of the text. The press is well aware of this inclination. The text—as reported by correspondents on the scene —often is not exciting enough to sell papers.

Finally, near the end of September, the journalists broke away from the capital and visited the village of Sam Teu in Samneua Province ten miles from the North Vietnamese border, where the government had reported heavy fighting. Laotian communiqués had said that Sam Teu had changed hands four times in five days of fierce combat.

The journalists inspected, and the truth at last became obvious.

"Correspondents," wrote Greg MacGregor of the *New York Times*, on September 22, "reported from the scene that Sam Teu was practically unscathed and quoted the local commander as saying it had never been occupied by the rebels."

The next day the Laotian government banned the newspaperman from further travel.

Hanson Baldwin in writing a news summary for the same paper, said, ". . . it is now clear that the 'war' in Laos is very small, indeed, and that more bullets have been flying in the Laotian government briefings than at some of the outpost camps in the jungles . . ."

Eventually, a United Nations investigation team made a survey of the combat areas. They made a similar report: *no invasion, and precious little war.*

This is a far different story than we had been getting for three months. In the eyes of the world, the United States looked very foolish, at best, and very dangerous at worst.

You and I (and the highest officials in the land) formed our opinions from headlines, hearsay, and propaganda. We failed to read the complete reports as published in a *few* (very few) of the better newspapers. And we failed to recognize what should have been obvious—that the information we were believing was foreign propaganda. Our embassy people in Vientiane were duped worse than anyone. The American ambassador said, "We've got the situation zeroed in. We are closer to the Lao officials than we were to Magsaysay."

Certainly no one in America had the curiosity, courage, or intelligence to inquire about the big deception until very late in the game.

The American government, the American press, and you and I along with them, swallowed *The Big Deception from Laos,* hook, line, and sinker; and when the truth appeared at last, we made scarcely a gulp of protest.

Today, as I am adding a few extra paragraphs to this, the pendulum of Laotian politics has swung from pro-west down through neutralism. Coup d'états jump back and forth; but the Laos government has been steadily moving to the left. The newspapers tell about large quantities of Communist guns and supplies being airlifted into Vietnam. This I believe. But the Lao government's stories of seven North Vietnamese battalions, for these I want an American eye-witness account—that is, if we have anyone who can tell a Lao from a Kha from a Vietnamese.

And so, after ten years of direct and indirect efforts to save Laos, this once-cooperative nation seems to be slipping through our fingers. We are not losing it to armed aggression. (If that should come, it simply is the last blow.) In part, Laos has been spirited away from us by inexpensive subversion and down-to-earth politics. But mostly we have thrown away our good will and political strength by an ignorance which led to false confidence and corruption. We have clumsily alienated potential supporters by neglecting them for a few "pets," and have repelled others by maladroitness. The Communists, speaking native dialects, have found support among the masses while our elite "pets" turned out to be weak reeds. The Reds simply have taken advantage of our crass mistakes, the worst of which is our trying to substitute dollars for knowledge. By allowing corruption to flourish, we have shaken the fruit into Communist hands.

It is with shame and humiliation that we must admit that rich, talented America has competed unsuccessfully with the Reds in nonviolent combat. Neither the U. S. Foreign Service, nor any other U. S. agency, had produced knowledgeable, language-trained men to go into the Laotian jungles and mountains to work with the people. Worse yet, we either were ignorant of the facts—or we were incompetent to evaluate an obvious situation.

And most immoral of all—the government and press have not been honest with us. Officials hid their mistakes and simultaneously claimed nonexistent successes. Perhaps they were ashamed? Perhaps they had no faith in the toughness of the American people? Or feared America's reaction to truth? Or perhaps they just did not know.

All news sources used here are unclassified and easily available to private citizens. They are from articles pub-

lished in: Associated Press, Reuters, Time *Magazine,* Life, *United Press International, the* Wall Street Journal, *Reports from Congressional hearings,* The Reader's Digest, Newsweek, U. S. News and World Report, *State Department bulletins, United Nations pamphlets, and various newspapers, including the* New York Times.

2

The Editor from Thailand

RICH and happy, Thailand lies to the west of Laos, across the Mekong River. Their common border snakes back and forth for about a thousand miles. From Bangkok, Red China is a short bomber-flight to the north; and Thailand's other neighbors include turbulent Cambodia, Burma and Malaya.

Thailand lives in a troubled area of the world. Yet for hundreds of years she has remained free, independent, and reasonably prosperous. This accomplishment has been managed mostly by skillfully bending to every strong political wind. Thailand—which means "land of the free"—offends no one and tries to please all. In the meanwhile, although appearing to kowtow, she does what she jolly well pleases; and her people eat well.

In 1941 she defended herself against Japan for a full four hours—just to put on a good show and look brave; she then surrendered with honor and became a Japanese puppet. Thailand later even declared war on the United States.

In 1945 Thailand, with the wind blowing from a new quarter, deserted Japan and aligned herself with the victorious United States. Between then and now, she has permitted a grateful America to pour hundreds of millions of dollars of assistance into that happy, happy land.

The wily Thais, always merry and entertaining, gently and unobtrusively utilize every trick to enrich themselves and improve their positions. For example, almost all of the merchandise and equipment sent to Laos for the U. S. foreign aid program had to go through Thailand. About $60 million of this, one way or another, went into Thai pockets.

The brains of the country—the upper-class Thais—are, in my opinion, one of the best-educated, sophisticated, shrewd, and urbane ruling groups in the world. Their gentle cleverness is almost irresistible; and I know of only two American officials who have not succumbed to it. One, John Peurifoy, saw into the very guts of Thailand from the first day he became ambassador. (Not too long afterwards he was killed in a strange automobile accident. Some of my Thai friends believe he was murdered. But that's another story.)

One of the cleverest of the Thai brain-trusts is a newspaper editor. At home in Bangkok, he pulls no punches. In fact, once he was put in jail for printing insulting remarks about an American ambassador. This Thai is a brilliant editor, scintillating, cosmopolitan, and a very cultured gentleman indeed. He is as much at home at

American baseball games as he is in British clubs, German passion plays, Philippine cock-fights, or a meeting of learned professors discussing the genesis of the Thai language. Foreigners seek his company. His urbane, witty, and multi-lingual conversation is a joy to hear. Also, incidentally, he is an influential member of the Royal Thai family. He is a prince.

He is known for his occasional sarcastic outbursts, in print and out.

Several years ago, the editor was offered an all-expenses-paid trip to the United States by an American foundation. All he had to do was lecture about Thailand. He accepted. On his way to San Francisco, he stopped for a few days in Hawaii.

In Honolulu, a woman interested in international affairs invited some fifty people to her home to hear the editor discuss Thailand and show a movie he had made. (Incidentally, it was a remarkable movie, the work of an artist.)

When the editor began to talk to this little group of intelligentsia, he was sharp, sarcastic, and to the point. "Well," I thought to myself, "we are in for a wonderful evening. The old boy is in good form."

But, after about five minutes, he changed his melody. The vitality went out of his talk. His attitude became gentle and patronizing. Instead of slashing (as he had started), he now told how effective all the American representatives were in Thailand. He described how their efforts were driving the Communists back; and that the United States had nothing to worry about in Thailand. Everything was just peachy.

I listened in silence. I knew that there were many problems in Thailand; and I might have brought them out by asking questions, but I preferred to hear his vaudeville act all the way through. Also, there was something more important that I wanted to find out. When the evening was over, I invited the editor and Cal Scollon, the able and knowledgeable director of the Pacific and Asian Affairs Council, to my home.

After two drinks, I said to the editor, "Look, why did you lie to those people? You know damned well that the Americans in Thailand have a lot to learn—you told me so yourself. You know that the Thai government under Pibul Songgram is corrupt. You know that Communist merchandise is being sold throughout the land. You also know that Thailand is working herself into a position so that she can jump either way politically, exactly as she did in 1939 and again in 1945.

"Just why did you soft-soap my friends?"

The Thai editor slowly lifted his glass to his lips. The motion was relaxed.

"I am a Buddhist," he said gently, "I don't like to hurt the feelings of strangers. The people I spoke to this evening were kind to me. They were extending hospitality and friendship. Why should I shock them?

"I told your friends what they wanted to hear. That everything is beautiful. Suppose I told them the true state of affairs? What could those good people do about it anyway? They wouldn't even have understood it. It would have been a dull evening. Now, at least, they are happy. Is that not the Buddhist way to heaven?"

The editor illustrated his point with another story. It seems that a few years ago the United States wanted to make sure that the foreign aid which was being delivered to Thailand was of the proper type and volume to benefit the people. The United States government, according to the editor, made arrangements for a group of American anthropologists to live in Thailand for about a year and a half. The anthropologists planned to reside in a normal up-country village. During their eighteen-month residence in Thai homes, the anthropologists were to observe and research the needs of the Thai people. The American government would then have accurate information on which to base its foreign aid program.

"Well," the editor said, "of course, my government agreed entirely that this was a worthwhile project. Before the American college professors arrived, we found a little village in a healthy, comfortable location, and we evacuated all the inhabitants. Hand-picked Thai officials and their families were moved into this new "average community" and they were instructed how to act and what to tell the learned professors. And so, when these PhD's and their assistants left at the end of eighteen months, they knew what we wanted them to know. Their report confirmed the fact that American assistance was just about perfect. Everyone was happy, and the Thai aid program continued."

For the next few months, in his visit throughout the

United States, according to the press the Thai editor repeated soft-soap performances to satisfied audiences. He said that everything in Thailand was jolly; the Communists were being pushed back; that Americans stationed there were doing a superb job; and that it was totally unnecessary for an American in Thailand to speak any language except English.

The American press reported what the prince said. It was reported "straight." No reporter seemed to know enough to ask him questions. And—after all—he was a prince and an editor—he must be telling the truth.

Note For the Reader:

I showed this chapter to a lady from Thailand—an educated lady who is distantly related to the editor. Here are her comments.

"I hadn't heard about the anthropologists incident. But it's possible. There were some anthropologists from America who came to Thailand. But, as I said, I don't know the details of their visit. But he (the editor) has a brilliant imagination. He can make up convincing anecdotes to illustrate any point.

"I don't doubt that he (the editor) told audiences in America stories he had dreamed up . . . that it is unnecessary for Americans to learn our language . . . that the Communists are being decisively defeated . . . and a lot of other pipedreams. But don't blame the Prince (the editor). Blame yourselves. Your American audiences don't come to a lecture to get information. They come for entertainment. You Americans are the easiest country in the world to propagandize. You believe anything. I could give a lecture here in Honolulu and say that the King's mother has two heads, and that is why she isn't seen in public. Most of the audience would believe it and the papers probably would print it as a factual story—without even checking to see if His Majesty's mother is still alive. It makes me sad because you're such a wonderful people and such a pure nation."

3

What We Aren't Told about Formosa

"We want the question of peace or war for America to be decided by the Congress as the Constitution provides—not by Generalissimo Chiang Kai-shek."

—John F. Kennedy, September 16, 1959

FOR OVER 4,000 years China has been peopled by a race of lean, ambitious, and usually hungry people; a breed of vigorous warriors, industrious peasants, clever merchants, pragmatic philosophers, and wily politicians. The politicians of this mighty nation deserve special notice. More often than not, they have been ruthless manipulators for personal power who have been able to present a false image of themselves to the public. The image has been a pious one, that of a moralizing force, of a Confucian simplicity, of a democratic leadership. This play-acting, this political masquerade, is typically Chinese. Foreigners are puzzled by it; but every Chinese fully understands and is aware of the dual nature of his officials. As long as the charade remains within traditional bounds, the Chinese do not object.

Old Mother China has had her ups and downs. She has

been split and fractured by political intrigues and internecine struggles. She has bled from the wounds inflicted by marauding conquerers; she has been parched by cruel droughts which baked and cracked her rich earth, and her hungry people have from necessity swallowed bark and grass. She has nearly drowned in floods of her yellow, silted, raging rivers. But Old Mother China has survived for at least 4,000 years while young, surging countries have blown away like dandelion puffs in the gales of centuries. She has always been in forward motion. Her armies have marched, slain, and conquered. What her armies could not subjugate, her commerce and effective diplomacy masticated and assimilated.

For forty centuries the mysterious vitality of the Chinese people has remained a deep well of strength which has resisted internal rot and external attacks. For almost a hundred generations, nimble Chinese fingers, practical brains, and a talent for politics have passed from fathers to sons, from mothers to daughters, from prime ministers to prime ministers. With this has also come the patience to float above temporary frustrations and wait for the golden days of opportunity to reappear.

From the poorest to the richest, the Chinese have always been certain that they are the superior, the most rational, the most cultured people on earth; and four thousand years of recorded history has not refuted this concept. It is natural, then, for these yellow men to conclude that uncouth barbarians (everyone who is not Chinese) should be the footstools and rungs on which the children of China should wipe their feet and climb upward.

Chinese realize that occasionally some lucky barbarians

will blot out the Yellow Sun. But be patient, say the Chinese, in time we will chew, absorb, and get nourishment from these boors—be they Caucasians, Malays, or even Russians who are mixtures of every race. We will devour and use them. They are the compost from which we blossom.

To deal with more powerful barbarians may require the entire spectrum of Chinese guile, force, flattery, bribery, chicanery, and political legerdemain. Westerners may consider these methods immoral; but the Chinese see nothing wrong—for it is within their hearts to inherit the earth and assume their rightful place—above other men. Chinese instinctively strive for this. Without special stimulation they will work hard, swallow pride, and endure privations to gain further advantage and superiority. And the Chinese politician—he does these things with a gusto, a cruelty and cunning far beyond the understanding of most Americans, ambassadors and military leaders included.

What follows is the story of a politician named Chiang Kai-shek. He may have sometimes worn Western clothes, but in his mind and marrow vibrates the accumulation of 4,000 years of Chinese warlord sagacity, ruthlessness, and public piousness. By use of these techniques—assisted by his well-coordinated relatives—the politician Chiang has, during two-score years, enjoyed more than his share of earthly glory and riches. Even now, in adversity—cooped up on the tiny island of Formosa, his strength gone, his political machinery rusted away, his once vast armies dissipated—even now he struts and crows, telling the world that he ultimately will regain those things so dear to him:

power over vast China and the concommitant riches. But being completely Chinese, his grasping-for-power is done in the name of public morality. In this instance it is called democracy and freedom, two things about which this politician knows nothing; nor has he ever practiced their principles. Yet so skillful are he and his family at political charades that for decades he has used freedom-loving America as the golden compost from which he derived nourishment and protection.

Let us look at this clever fellow, Chiang Kai-shek, now pacing, scolding, and intriguing on small, overcrowded Formosa, a hundred miles off the coast of China's mainland.

Americans were dupes on events occurring in Laos. We didn't even know its geographical location—let alone what was happening. But with Chiang Kai-shek we believe we are quite familiar. Countless news items have been written on him and his country by American journalists; and many of our politicians have shouted their lungs out on Sino-American problems. Our bookstores bulge with material concerning China and the Generalissimo. His wife went to Wellesley—and had spent much time in America where her family owns rich properties and vast investments.

Still, certain important facts may have escaped us; or perhaps they were hidden from us; or perhaps we just forgot.

Who remembers the 1920's when Chiang Kai-shek started public life as a close associate of the Communists? Or when he went to Moscow to "meet Lenin, Trotzky and Chicherin, to study Bolshevist strategy, ideology, and revolutionary technique, and to seek aid of a material nature from Moscow."*

Chiang Kai-shek's first leap to power and fame was made with Communist assistance; and although the Generalissimo was not a Red, he remained in bed with them as long as he thought they could help him.

But when conservative Shanghai bankers, in panic over Communism's growth, volunteered to finance Chiang—providing he ceased being a radical—Chiang grabbed the opportunity. Dumping his Red associates, he became a respectable anti-Communist. At the same time, he latched on to the coattails and petticoats of the powerful and rich Soong family. He did this by marrying the spinster daughter, Mei-ling, the Wellesley graduate.

The Soongs—with Chiang as their front man—rode the back of China for twenty years. Every senior member of the Soong clan, except Madame Sun Yat-sen, had important strategic posts in the government. And in the process they became one of the wealthiest families in the world.

But during those twenty years, Chiang's China grew more corrupt and poverty-stricken even than under the infamous warlord rulers. As the common man groaned under excessive abuses, so did Chiang's regime become more and more totalitarian.

At the end of World War II, most Americans at home believed the Generalissimo to be a genius, a man of Confucian wisdom, a brave saviour of his country; a fighter for democracy and freedom. However, the Chinese people felt otherwise. They hated the Generalissimo, neither be-

* H. F. McNair, *China in Revolution*, p. 99.

lieving nor respecting him. The people finally rejected him because they were sick of him and the Soongs. The nation was ripe for a take-over—the rotten Chinese apple was ready to drop on its own accord. Some people doubt this, and the accusation has been made that America's failure to give Chiang sufficient military aid is what caused his downfall and handed China to the Reds. Such conclusions are based on ignorance, propaganda and gullibility. Actually, in 1945, Chiang had billions of dollars of U. S. equipment for his three-million-man army. But his troops had neither the training nor the will-to-fight for Chiang's regime. Money for their food and their pay (supplied by USA) went into pockets of officers. The majority of the troops were unwilling conscripts (as early as 1941 I personally have seen long lines of conscripts chained together on their way from their villages to training camps) who had no loyalty to Chiang. Many dissatisfied Chinese troops voluntarily turned their ammunition and supplies over to the Communists.

During these difficult times the government of Chiang Kai-shek and his relatives, the Soongs and the Kungs, continued to take over more and more businesses. In early 1947 even the UNRRA food earmarked for a starving populace was sold at obscene prices in the black market. No wonder the people listened to the Communists. They were willing to take a chance on anything for a change.

All kinds of false excuses are offered for Chiang's being thrown out of China. Some apologists say that Communists wormed their way into power under the protective title of "agrarian reformers." The fact is, the Communists denied this title. In 1940–1941 I had many lengthy conversations with Chou En-lai. He laughed at the "agrarian reformers" legend; and said, "If you want a political label for us, call us Communists. Revolutionaries. Marxists."

Mao Tse-tung, in a lengthy speech, also publicly ridiculed the "agrarian reformer" myth.

It was Chiang himself who created the "agrarian reformers" tale. His manufacturing of this tremendous lie occurred in the 1939–1940 period when he was trying to get a loan from the United States. With his tongue in his cheek, Chiang wrote to Secretary of the Treasury Morgenthau that there were no Communists left in China; and the opposition party simply were agrarian reformers. I was in Chungking at that time and saw how Chiang's censors deleted the word "Communists" and substituted "agrarian reformers" in press dispatches.

The immensity of this untruth is staggering. At that time there were at least half a million well-armed, well-trained, and well-organized Reds up north; and Red propagandist units were successfully penetrating every province of China. I personally watched them at work within twenty miles of Chungking.

But facts meant nothing to Chiang, the Chinese politician. He officially passed the same "agrarian reformer" canard to the British ambassador, Sir Archibald Clark-Kerr; and announced in a press conference, "There are no Communists in China." Even his American propaganda adviser, Earl Leaf, wrote U. S. correspondents requesting that they "stop calling Chu Teh, Mao Tse-tung, and others, Communists."

So great was Chinese censorship and news suppression during this period that I doubt whether even the U. S. government fully understood the events of the early '40's. A foreign-service officer in Chungking seriously told me that there was nothing to fear from the ridiculous handful of "agrarian reformers." Madame Chiang Kai-shek personally had assured him that Mao Tse-tung, Chou En-lai, and Chu Teh were nothing but petty bandits who, in a few years, would be forgotten.

Eight years later, these "petty bandits" were masters of 700,000,000 Chinese; and Chiang Kai-shek had fled China, beaten and confused. But he and his relatives, the Soongs, had gotten their personal fortunes and the government gold reserves out first. There wasn't even enough cash left to pay the few loyal troops who remained behind to fight a rear-guard action to protect Chiang's escape.

The legend of Chiang Kai-shek's military brilliance is a myth; but the myth has taken such a firm hold in gullible America that a recent Chairman of the Joint Chiefs of Staff (in answer to a newspaperman's question, in my presence) said, "The Generalissimo is the greatest military genius of our time."

The fact is that, on his own, Generalissimo Chiang Kai-shek has never won a major military campaign. His famous 1926 northern campaign, on which his military reputation was established, was managed by Communist propagandists who were assisting him.

After his flight from China, over twenty years later, Chiang sought refuge and safety in Formosa, where today he brashly assures his American advisers that he still is the boss of all China and that the Chinese people fervently wish for his return.

But even his escape to Formosa was a botched-up job. Chiang's armies pillaged and robbed Formosa when they first arrived. Stores were looted. Hospitals were gutted, their pipes and electrical fixtures ripped out and sold. When the Formosans objected, Chiang's armies resorted to their machine-guns. Thousands of Formosans were slaughtered.

It is barely a decade since Chiang's Chinese armies murdered and oppressed the Formosans who, at first, had given them welcome and refuge. It takes almost a pathological desire for self-deception to assume the Formosans have forgotten this mass-murder and thievery so quickly. A warped imagination is required to believe that Formosans, only ten years after, now love the Chiang Kai-shek government. Can anyone in a single decade develop affection for the killers of his relatives and neighbors?

The Formosans are bitter on the subject of Chiang Kai-shek—a regime which they do not want (they don't want the Communists either). I have seen Formosans grimace with anger when they hear Americans repeat the yarn that when Chiang arrived he found an ignorant, backward, and medieval populace in Formosa; and that by brilliant leadership he transformed the previously miserable island into an educated, skilled, and happy community.

Of course this is false. Under the Japanese the Formosans were colonials, but they were 95% literate. Their agricultural techniques were the most advanced in Asia—with the exception of Japan. True, there have been land reforms (mostly the breaking up of old Japanese estates) and agricultural developments during the last ten years; but the literacy and inherited skill were present long before Chiang Kai-shek sought refuge there. Under the Japanese, the island of Formosa had been well developed technically. The entire area had been laced with a modern and efficient network of good roads, irrigation, and electrification.

Anyone who visits Formosa today will see relative prosperity and the gay sparkle of economic upsurge. But the fact remains that the 9,000,000 Formosans still intensely dislike the 2,000,000 Chinese Nationalists refugees who are in power over them; and the Formosans prefer an independent nation for Formosans. They look with a cool eye to America; and they blame us for holding the Chinese on their backs. Which, of course, is a justified criticism from their point of view. They emphasize that Formosa does not belong to Chiang Kai-shek; and, incidentally, President Truman when in office confirmed their opinion.

Most Americans believe that Formosa belongs to the Chinese Nationalists. This is not so. After World War II the great powers decided that the status of Formosa would be determined at *some future date*. Chiang squats there because he has no other place to go.

Another false belief is that the freedom-loving Nationalists have made Formosa into a political Utopia which is an example for all of Asia to follow—that there are fair elections; and that officials are elected by a democratic process. On a local level they are. But in choosing men at the top—the equivalent of our Congress—the common people have no voice. Here is where the policy-making power rests; and the several thousand top legislators who were appointed arbitrarily by Chiang Kai-shek via a rigged election in 1948 still hold the same positions. Almost all of them are Chinese refugees, not native Formosans who constitute 80% of the population.

If Formosans had the opportunity of nominating and voting for members of the National Assembly, the chances are that Chiang Kai-shek and his entourage would be thrown out of office.

The Chinese Nationalists are sustained in Formosa by Americans, and perhaps for excellent reasons. However, it is an expensive operation. Directly and indirectly, the U. S. probably spends about three-quarters of a billion dollars a year defending and upholding Chiang Kai-shek. The State Department and Department of Defense will not permit American citizens to know the cost, so we can only estimate. But including the cost of maintaining U. S. military strength there, the amount is tremendous.

The American politicians and military leaders who justify the cash given to Chiang claim that the patriotic army of Nationalist China is young, well-trained, and of high morale. The implication is clear: the Nationalist army would fight to the last man in the effort to defeat Red China. Of course, this can never be known for sure until the moment of battle, but any military man with a sense of history realizes that an army made up of young Formosans conscripted into military service against their desires and under the domination of foreigners probably will be ineffective in combat.

The fact is that about 70% of the *young* men in the Chinese Nationalist military are Formosan conscripts. They have no interest in recapturing the mainland of China for Chiang Kai-shek. In *defensive* combat they probably would battle well. But if Chiang's army were to invade China, my prediction is that the majority of his troops would mutiny, or simply hang back and not fight.

The assertion that Chiang's army is a potent weapon is poppycock based mostly on (1) the theatrical mock-combat shows which one crack unit puts on for visitors; (2) the statements of U. S. military officers who are training Chinese troops and who, as a matter of policy and diplomacy, cannot say depreciative things about their students in public; (3) the successful "shoot-downs" which the Chinese Air Force has had over the Communists. Even these are not an accurate yardstick of quality in depth. A military machine's total effectiveness cannot be measured by the operations of a few "stars." Neither, incidentally, can a potential enemy be judged as incompetent by the few bad performances they make in peacetime. Great Britain and the United States learned this expensive lesson in the war against Japan. Warriors who had been regarded as little, bow-legged men with thick glasses and supposedly inferior equipment surprised everyone. They showed up in combat with a frighteningly high effectiveness. When Japanese planes bombed Manila, the U. S. military and naval attachés could not believe such accuracy possible. They assumed, publicly, that the planes were being flown by German pilots. America's ignorance in international affairs is nothing new.

Regrettably, the 500,000-man military organization of Chiang Kai-shek would be of not-too-great use in an all-out war with Red China. *It would be the United States which would assume the brunt of the fighting.* Actually the Chinese Nationalists only need a small army.

The real reason for maintaining a 500,000-man Nationalist military machine is twofold: First, it is an excuse to get money from the United States. We support the bulk of that army; and if it were dissolved, there would be a national economic problem. How else could several hundred thousand Chinese who have no other source of income or trade be supported?

Secondly, the presence of such a large military department permits Chiang to maintain a complete dictatorship over the island.

Chiang Kai-shek could not last a month without our support. Despite this, the Nationalists privately are annoyed at the United States. First, they do not enjoy being dependent upon someone else's charity—especially if there are thousands of the benefactors (and their families) present to remind them. Second, the Chinese have lived a life of frustration and despair on Formosa for over ten years now. They have seen their chances of regaining power on the mainland become dimmer and dimmer. Whether we like it or not, they are getting perilously close to the end of their rope. *Probably the only thing which can save them is a World War III in which America opposes Communist China.* This, for the last five years, has been Chiang's chief objective. He believes America owes this to him.

The Chinese Nationalists have mesmerized themselves into believing that if it were not for America's restrictions, they long ago would have regained control of the mainland of China. From Chiang down, they secretly vent their spleen on America. Occasionally their wrath bursts out for all to see—for example, the sacking of the American Embassy in Taipei on May 24, 1957. This incident has some facets worth thinking about.

The genesis of the riot was when a Chinese Nationalist named Liu was found murdered outside the quarters of an American G.I. The G.I. was accused of the crime and brought to trial in a U. S. Army court-martial.

Testifying that the dead man, Liu, had been a "peeping Tom," the G.I. said that Liu had sneaked up to his house and watched his wife taking a bath. In order to insure his wife's safety, the G.I. ran outside to chase the "peeping Tom" away. There was a struggle. Liu, the Chinese, attacked the soldier with a club. In self-defense, the G.I. shot him (so testified the G.I.).

There was a lengthy court-martial. It was open to the public; and members of the Chinese Department of Justice attended. These representatives of Chiang Kai-shek publicly said the trial was unfair. The murderer of a Chinese was getting a whitewash job. As a result of this official rabble-rousing, there was considerable rancor and dissatisfaction in the Chinese newspapers. The full significance of this can only be grasped upon recognizing that the press in Taipei is almost completely under governmental influence. Within the last fifteen years, there has only been one vigorous dissenting periodical; and its editor is now in jail for ten years.

The G.I. was acquitted; and the Chinese press screamed that a grave injustice had been done. Americans, they said, could abuse Chinese and get away with it.

Not many days after the trial, the widow of the dead Chinese, Liu, appeared before the American Embassy carrying a big placard complaining of the injustice of the trial. The sign was printed in English. But Mrs. Liu did not speak or write English.

A small crowd gathered. Within an hour a thousand Chinese packed the street. An officer of the official Chinese Broadcasting Service showed up with a tape-recorder. Mrs. Liu read a *prepared* speech into the microphone. She did this with considerable histrionics. When her impassioned complaints were finished, the official Chinese newscaster turned the volume of his recorder up to the maximum, and played the speech back for the crowd to hear. The crowd turned into an angry mob and began breaking into the Embassy.

The Embassy was totally wrecked—even to the point where the safes were broken open. Communist newspapers and radio broadcasts all over the world laughed at our embarrassment. America, indeed, looked foolish and politically inept.

There are several odd coincidences connected with this event. Why, in a police state, did not Chiang Kai-shek's security troops break up the mob and stop them from gutting the U. S. Embassy? The amazing fact is that the troops had been removed from Taipei for that day. They were outside the city on an air-raid drill. This had been planned to take place earlier; but had been delayed, one day at a time, until the riot. But even so there was a shed-full of Chinese army tanks a few blocks away. Why were they not used?

Actually, it was common knowledge around Taipei that there would be a demonstration at the U. S. Embassy on that morning. The evening before the trouble started, several Catholic priests, for example, received mysterious telephone calls. "Please, father, don't go on the streets tomorrow morning. And by all means stay away from the American Embassy."

The priests I discussed this with said they each had received about half a dozen such warnings. *This was the day before the riot occurred.*

A Formosan doctor assured me he had heard details 48 hours beforehand. Almost everyone—except the Americans —had known about it.

My Chinese friends told me that for a week, children in Taipei schools had been lectured about American Imperialism. They had been given plans and instructions on how they would assemble and march to the U. S. Embassy. It appears obvious that every detail of the ruckus had been decided beforehand by the Nationalist government. Everyone except Americans seemed to know all the details.

The third odd coincidence was that the riot occurred shortly after the American ambassador had left Taipei for a vacation in Hongkong; and that the U. S. government officials had no inkling of the approaching holocaust— even though the local population was thoroughly prepared.

The fourth strange circumstance is that pictures were made by Chinese news photographers of the mob breaking into the Embassy. Ringleaders were identified as members of Chiang Ching-kuo's secret police. Chiang Ching-kuo is the Generalissimo's oldest son—who lived in Moscow for several years and is married to a Soviet Russian wife. To-day this Russian-trained son is the second most influential man in Formosa. He is chief of the secret police as well as dictator of the political commissars who dominate the military; and he is boss of various youth organizations. He speaks better Russian than he does Formosan or English; in fact, two years ago he spoke no English or Formosan at all. My friends in Taipei tell me he is the only official in the Nationalist government who has not been made to sign an anti-Communist pledge.

Within a matter of days, every newspaper which had published pictures of Ching-kuo's men—and every copy of the picture—mysteriously disappeared.

To add to the witch's brew, two highly placed Chinese Foreign Office officials told me additional bits of shocking information.

"We have every reason to believe," said the Chinese officials, "that Liu (the man who was killed) and the American G.I. were close associates. They even knew each other's wives. We had a strong case that Liu and the American had been in black-market operations together; and that Liu owed the American considerable money. We heard that the American was about to be ordered out of Formosa and was clamoring for his cash.

"Our medical examiner told us that the stick found near

Liu's body was so small it could not inflict bodily harm on anyone; and that the second bullet had entered Liu's back, from a distance of about thirty feet—thus indicating that he had been shot while running away."

I said, "If you had circumstantial evidence, or even just rumors about these things, why didn't you tell the U. S. prosecution?"

The Chinese officials both said that they had purposely withheld the information. The Republic of China and the United States were about to renegotiate a status-of-forces agreement; and it would have been to the advantage of the Chinese to establish the fact that the American courts are not fair. The Chinese were trying to use the trial (and the demonstration) as a political instrument.

This is not the picture you and I had of the Formosa riot. Yet we had hundreds of American officials in Formosa whose major job was to know what was happening. Also the Associated Press had an experienced representative there whose responsibility it was to inform the United States. He did not. The United Press reporter, a young man named Brown, described the events leading up to the riots and, as a result found himself ostracized by both American and Chinese officials. He was accused of irresponsibility and of "pink" leanings.

Our untrue image of the incident is a triumph of Chiang's propaganda machine which, generally, for about twenty years, has been able to lead America around by the nose.

Chiang is well aware of the Hitler maxim that if you say the same thing over and over in many ways, the public may eventually accept it. The Chinese Nationalists have, through our press and government, bombarded us with unconfirmed accounts of Red invasions, of exaggerated stories of build-ups for invasions, and of unverified descriptions of internal revolutions within Communist China.

Between accounts of "imminent attacks," the Nationalists' public-relations officials have cranked out endless yarns which extol the strength and efficiency of Chiang Kai-shek's army, navy, and air force. These yarns confidentially claim that the Nationalists can defeat Red China single-handedly; all that is needed is American equipment and logistic support. They brag of how popular the Nationalists are in Formosa; and of how the Chinese Communist bubble is about to burst.

These flim-flam stories are given to newspapermen in mimeographed hand-outs; they are told to visiting dignitaries in official briefings; they are whispered in confidential tones by Madame Chiang Kai-shek to tourist groups coming to Formosa.

Whether the accounts are untrue is not the important issue. It is the unquestioning acceptance of them by you and me, by most of our press and government, which is the tragic factor.

The thoroughness with which the Nationalists (and other countries also) make suckers of us is fantastic.

For example, shortly after we heard about the Red Chinese system of communes, an American journalist wrote a highly publicized article on that subject. It exuded scholarship and authenticity. A large part of his story was based on an interview with a Chinese who had escaped from a Communist commune. I happened to be in Hong-kong about this time, and tracked down the alleged Chinese eyewitness to the commune system. As soon as I met him I recognized him as an acquaintance from Formosa. He was a propagandist employed by the Nationalist government.

This fellow had been planted in Macao to pose as a refugee. His job was to tell English-speaking tourists and journalists about atrocities he had seen and experienced in Red China.

I am not denying that the communes are a frightful thing. The thought of their ultimately being successful fills me with apprehension; because if 700,000,000 Chinese ever are efficiently harnessed, China probably could out-produce the United States two to one.

We should know about communes. We should know everything possible about China. But we should have this information in perspective and cradled in truth—not via the medium of foreign propaganda or journalism which is trying to prove a point or fertilize a headline. We should study communes not as something immoral (which permits us to feel pious and superior) but as a foreign economic weapon which is a danger to our country.

America has a few competent newspaper reporters who are experts on Asia and who speak Chinese. It is from their *personal observations* in China that we should learn about communes. A few years ago Red China invited them to look around. But our Secretary of State refused them permission. Now all that we know about the largest nation in the world—official and unofficial—is either second-hand or classified. Yet, we have seldom complained about our incompetent and incomplete information-gathering system. When Dulles stopped reporters from going to China, the American press could have forced him to change his decision. They failed. After a few weak wails they quieted down and went back to the job of selling newspapers.

I cannot recall a single major issue concerning Formosa on which we have received a steady flow of accurate information and counsel. For example, we have been given a dose of unrealistic accounts on the offshore islands of Quemoy and Matsu. We have been told (1) They are essential to the defense of Formosa, and (2) If Chiang is forced to remove his troops from these islands that the morale of Formosa—and Free Chinese all over the world—will collapse.

I disagree; and I am in good company. When the placing of Nationalist troops on Quemoy and Matsu began, the move was considered contrary to the best interests of the United States. Both the Department of State and the Joint Chiefs of Staff opposed Chiang's maneuver.

In 1958 President Eisenhower said in a press conference, "I believe, as a soldier, that was not a good thing to do, to have all those troops there."

Assistant Secretary of State Walter Robertson said, "It is not really anyone above the intelligence of a military moron who would for one moment think that these islands would be selected as bases from which to attack the mainland."

In September 1958 former Secretary of State Acheson

described Chiang's intention as "to embroil the United States with his enemies the Communists."

It seems strange then that although the United States *had the authority to stop Chinese troops* from being stationed on Quemoy and Matsu (The Dulles-Yeh letters), we did nothing to prevent it. Chiang Kai-shek simply outmaneuvered and outsmarted us. At that time there were rumors spread that the Chinese Communists had made peace offers to Formosa. The unspoken implication was that Chiang was considering them if the United States did not back him on Quemoy and Matsu. Blackmail. This is an old play for Chiang. He played the same trick during World War II. When the Roosevelt administration differed with him, Chiang let it be known that Japan had suggested a separate peace with China. If he did not get the assistance he demanded from America, the morale of his people would collapse; and he would have to accept the Japanese peace offer. P.S.—Chiang's demands were fulfilled.

Today, by bluff, by dividing the opposition, by propaganda, the clever Chiang has done it again. Today we are awkwardly entangled in the offshore islands; and Chiang Kai-shek has almost manipulated us to their total defense —even though our treaty calls only for the defense of Formosa and the Pescadores.

If we had been well-informed and firm in 1956 this dilemma could have been avoided. Today we are in an awkward diplomatic and military position—but don't forget, Eisenhower made the deal with the tacit approval of the American public.

Let us analyze the Quemoy situation realistically. First,

consider the claim that tiny Quemoy and Matsu (3 miles from Red China) are absolutely necessary for the defense of Formosa. These tiny specks—almost contiguous to Red China—are they needed for the security of Formosa, which is over a hundred miles away? Examine the map carefully. Red China has approximately 300 miles of convenient coastline suitable for launching ships or planes for an invasion.

Certainly it is not 80,000 Nationalist soldiers on two spit-kit islands which would stop a Communist onslaught. They could be by-passed without trouble. Or, if necessary, they could be overwhelmed by the vast assets of Communist China and her 700,000,000 population. Furthermore, without the logistic support of the U. S. Navy, the troops on Quemoy and Matsu would starve and run out of ammunition.

I cannot emphasize too much that it is not the Nationalist strength—be they on Quemoy or Formosa—which is thwarting the Communists. The Nationalist effort couldn't hold out a month alone against a determining Communist attack. It is the U. S. Seventh Fleet which deters the initial military aggression.

The Chinese have little to fear from Chiang Kai-shek's forces. It is the U. S. Navy, U. S. Army, U. S. Air Force, and U. S. Marines which ultimately would throw back an invasion. The occupation of Quemoy and Matsu by Chiang's troops is almost of no military significance. Chiang simply is using it as a political vise in which to squeeze and hold the United States.

Although they are of no military importance, these three-miles-from-China islands are of considerable *propaganda* value. Regrettably most of the propaganda advantages go to the Communists.

The Chinese Communists are in an advantageous position, and they are making the most of the people's indignation. It is one of the finest propaganda weapons the Reds have for internal use. China is hard-pressed. There have been severe crop failures. The Five Year plan has not gone along as well as expected. The communes system backfired. To keep the people's minds off the failures at home, the Chinese leaders must stir the masses into a constant state of anxiety and fear of foreign devils. Quemoy and Matsu are rich sources of the needed fear. By our own role in supporting Chiang there, we provide the Communists with precisely what they need.

In 1959 I interviewed Chinese refugees who had fled from Communist China to Hongkong. Without exception, they all had one thing to say: that the whip which drives the Chinese people to almost superhuman work efforts is hate and dread of America. The government tells them that America is getting ready to invade China; and that America is getting ready to drop nuclear bombs on China. Therefore, in order to survive, everyone must bend to Communist demands and slave in communes.

The fact that America supports Nationalists in Quemoy and Matsu—two islands a mere rifle-shot from Red China —lashes the Chinese people into a frenzy. Such a situation is a propaganda windfall for the Communists.

The occupation of these islands also costs Chiang and the United States world sympathy. Wherever I have traveled, both in Asia, Europe and the Pacific, other countries believe that the holding-on to Matsu and Quemoy is unreasonable and provocative.*

The half-truths swallowed by the American public seem to be endless. Some of these phony stories have skeletons of fact, but are studded with small chunks of propaganda. These bits and chunks have a habit of accruing into giant false images.

An example of this occurred on March 28, 1960, when the United Press International sent pictures of Generalissimo and Madame Chiang Kai-shek to newspapers throughout the United States. The caption under them said, "Taipei—President Chiang Kai-shek won an expected landslide victory for re-election in the National Assembly last week . . ."

The caption is accurate enough for someone who is an expert on China. But the average reader inferred that Chiang had been brought back to office by a popular clamor. In the first place, the reader was not told that it was contrary to the Nationalist Constitution for the Generalissimo to serve as Chief of State again. Nor did the reader realize that members of the National Assembly who elected Chiang were his own appointees. In short, Chiang Kai-shek simply decided that, contrary to the constitution, he would continue as dictator in Formosa—and to heck with what the people think about it. There had been much discussion about this by the Chinese and Formosan people

* For anyone desiring to make a detailed and documented study of the question, read "The Quemoy Imbroglio: Chiang Kai-shek and the United States" by Tang Tsen, University of Chicago, printed in *The Western Political Quarterly*, December 1959.

—mostly in private. My Chinese friends told me that public opinion in Formosa was against Chiang's retaining office and violating the constitution.

I discussed this incident with a high U. S. official; and then I told him all I knew about the general substance of this chapter on Formosa.

"Yes," he responded, "there is truth in everything you have told me. But do not write about it. Why wash our dirty linen in public? It hurts our allies and it aids the Communists."

I violently disagree with this thesis. If the American citizens know the truth—no matter how unpleasant—they will react with common sense. Our allies and the Communists already know the facts on Formosa. It is only the United States public which has allowed itself to be deceived.

At present it is our national policy to defend and support Chiang Kai-shek and the Soong family which has grown rich from him.

If we are to use a rascal, let us do it honestly and with our eyes open. Such has not been the case with Chiang Kai-shek and China. The American nation, in my opinion, has permitted itself to be dangerously led astray. Not only have American citizens allowed themselves to be stuffed with errors on the China issue; but in many instances they have been frightened away from exercising the boldest and proudest of American traditions: the privilege of saying what they think. Those few who have questioned United States actions in China—right or wrong—frequently have been accused of Communist leanings.

For the last twenty years it has been considered almost a sin to question the publicized image of Chiang Kai-shek and his billionaire family; and woe to anyone who disputes the glorious picture. There have been a few hesitant queries; but these have been drowned out by shouts of ill-informed politicians and a horde of skilled Chinese public-relations operators. The brutal truth about the Chinese issue seldom has been adequately presented; and the free press* of the United States has contributed more than its share to the discord and confusion.

We can only conclude that many officials (in government and out) either have been ignorant of conditions, or have been more concerned in molding public opinion and backing the administration than in providing citizens with honest facts.

If the present propaganda hocus-pocus—and the dumb sheeplike acceptance of everything by citizens—continues, I predict a difficult future for the United States of America. A great nation cannot survive for long on a shifty and slippery foundation of self-deception and misinformation.

* "Press" includes newspapers, TV, radio, magazines, and other news vehicles.

4

What We Aren't Told about Korea

FOURTEEN years of American ignorance about Korea, its people, their land, their government, traditions, language, and above all, about their number-one man, Syngman Rhee, led inexorably to the civilian uprising which eventually forced the American-supported Rhee to flee the country. Communist propaganda made much of the fact that once more the masses had overthrown a Yankee tyrant.

The realities of Korea—which our civilian officials, our military, and our press did not know at first (and never did pass on to us) led us to support a corrupt, oppressive government until the inevitable happened.

To understand what happened, it is necessary to know much that was not made clear to us by our press or by our government.

I have been in the Korean winter, shivering and teeth chattering, my nostrils hurting from the cold, my fingers and toes numb. I saw elderly Korean women wearing comparatively scanty clothing, plodding through ice and snow in what looked like flimsy ballet slippers. Despite the fact that their nation was at war, their countryside bombed, their larders empty, their clothing inadequate, and the weather freezing, these women moved along cheerfully, their backs straight, their cheeks pink—refusing to acknowledge that all was not well with the world and themselves.

The Koreans are physically tough. They have the capacity for absorbing suffering and hardship without flinching, without emotion or fuss. To a Westerner sometimes it seems that they have no nerve endings.

Once in Seoul I was present when a Korean thief was caught stealing a pair of pants from an army truck. Brought before the Korean magistrate, the culprit was called upon to confess. He pleaded innocent. One by one, the magistrate had the thief's fingers broken in an effort to make him confess. He never did; and he submitted to the excruciating pain of physical mutilation without a murmur or complaint.

They are a fierce lot, these Koreans. Perhaps it is their rugged land and climate which has bred this quality into them. Even forty years of thorough Japanese colonialism did not subdue them. Underground revolutionary organizations quietly flourished. Korean literature, art and culture somehow progressed despite the Japanese strait-jacket.

The Koreans are experts—more than that, artists—at survival under severe conditions. As a result they are, when necessary, among the world's most accomplished thieves.

No well-buttoned pocket, no guarded and triple-locked storehouse is safe from their nimble fingers and risk-taking spirit. The Army of the United States can well attest to this.

So there we have them, thirty-two million tough, hardy, stubborn, spirited people. Their skin is like well-tanned leather; and their souls are like kegs of dynamite attached to a short, unpredictable fuse.

This, then, too, is Syngman Rhee—the old man whose dream it was to have a united, independent Korea with himself as the President. Don't forget that last phrase, *with himself as the President.*

Listen to Dr. Rhee, soft, persuasive and gentle when he discusses his dreams—and knows that everyone is listening with admiration. But when he is opposed, then his jaw muscles bunch spasmodically, the wide mouth opens like a steel trap, and violent accusations thunder out.

On September 8, 1945, thousands of Koreans milled through the streets of South Korean cities cheering, yelling joyously, waving flags, pounding each other on the back, and dancing. For forty years the oppressed Koreans had waited for this moment. And on this day it had happened. The U. S. Army under General Hodge had arrived (the Russian army, with no more notice than we had, had occupied North Korea three weeks earlier) to accept the Japanese surrender and to set up a temporary military government to tide the nation over until the war-turbulences and disorders were squared away. Now, at last, the

Japanese colonists and exploiters would be thrown out. Korea, which for thirteen hundred years had been a closely knit unit with one language, one race, and one culture, would again be free and independent.

The happy, half-starved Koreans thronged around the comfortable government buildings where the hated Japanese had lived and worked. Soon these would be filled with Korean patriots. In some instances the Korean crowds wanted to drag out the Japanese officials; but the presence of the Japanese army—even though Japan had surrendered —discouraged such violence. Then, too, there was the knowledge that General Hodge would take care of such matters with despatch and dignity.

Hodge, an able and energetic combat officer, had a thousand complicated civil tasks to perform immediately: initiating a food supply system, establishing local governments, the encouragement of a stable non-Communist Korean political setup, fishing regulations, the repatriation of Japanese, the appointing of officials to take over from the Japanese, the rebuilding of power plants, sewage disposal, water supply, re-establishing school systems, starting medical care—and the other countless functions necessary to a multimillion-people state.

All this had to be done at once. Cold weather was beginning and Korea was ill-prepared for either the winter or the political future. The nation temporarily was paralyzed by economic and administrative anarchy.

Various South Korean leaders and political groups were jockeying for power. No one really knew which leaders stood for what. In North Korea, the busy Russians, assisted by thousands of thoroughly indoctrinated and trained Korean Communists, were working hard to create confusion and thwart American efforts in the South.

It was urgent that a skeleton government be established —and fast. But General Hodge's staff was not trained to take over the administrative positions. They knew neither the Korean language nor the national format and needs. *The U. S. government had made no plans for occupying Korea.*

There was only one recognizable and operating organization available—the old, despised Japanese officials. Utilizing them temporarily, to keep things moving in the absence of able and trusted Korean elements, was the only thing Hodge could do. At this emotional and inflammable period in Korean history, nothing could have offended the Koreans more. When they heard General Hodge had ordered the continued use of Japanese officials, the populace almost went out of their minds. Were the Americans betraying them?

From the start there was tension and strain between the Americans and the prospective Korean leaders. And General Hodge, on instruction from MacArthur, stood distant from the few who had been trying to organize the government.

It was at this point—just five weeks after the U. S. Army's 24th Corps had occupied Korea—that Syngman Rhee arrived in Seoul. With deep emotion he breathed the chilly October air. He was seventy, and for almost a half century Rhee had been in America, patriotically plotting and dreaming of the day when he would liberate Korea and become chief of state. Now the opportunity had been born. The enthusiastic populace that cheered outside his hotel (after his arrival had been well publicized by the U. S. Army), gave Rhee the assurance that what he had long believed was true—that he, Syngman Rhee, was the only man who could lead Korea in this glorious but difficult era.

Wasting no time, he went to work. His first task was to have the Americans back him. He called on the American commanders. Speaking fluent English, he let them know he had a doctor's degree from Princeton; and claimed he had been a friend of Woodrow Wilson. The harried American administrators naturally were glad to meet any Westernized Korean in this strange land; and they listened to him. Rhee strengthened his position by hinting that other Korean leaders had Communist leanings. The Communist scare became his unfailing technique for gaining power— and for holding it, during his entire career. The U. S. Army, in the meanwhile, gave him privileges which were denied other leaders. He was allowed to broadcast on the Army's radio station, he had the use of a limousine, and he was guarded twenty-four hours a day by American GI's. *Without United States assistance it is unlikely that he would have come to power.*

In 1948 Rhee became the first president of the Republic of Korea. His cabinet was composed of his cronies; the United Nations Temporary Commission noted, "There was widespread criticism of the personnel appointed to the cabinet, and the feeling was expressed that the President had failed to utilize fully the best talents available." But Rhee paid no attention. He claimed that he, and he only, knew what was best for Korea.

During his first two years in Korea—as his power grew—he began to treat his American benefactors with a high hand. Rhee not only agitated for the withdrawal of U. S. military forces, but he embarrassed the American commander, General Hodge, by publicly charging him with building up the Communist Party and by telling tall tales —for example, his statement that the Department of State would bring about separate elections in South Korea—thus abandoning the idea of unification. The Department of State had made no such agreement or announcement. It appeared clear that although Rhee wanted U. S. economic, military, and political support, he still used America willy-nilly as a whipping-boy to further his own ends.

No Americans seemed to object; they accepted his rantings and unreasonable temper with passive obeisance. And so Rhee became more and more dictatorial in his lust for power; and in the meantime—even though he had been president only a year—he paid less and less attention to the details of administering Korea. Richard C. Allen in his book, *Korea's Syngman Rhee,* reports, "In the faction-ridden Assembly, various groups worked on behalf of the landowners and mining interests but almost no one for the welfare of Korea as a whole. Throughout the government, officials reverted to centuries-old practices in supplementing their meager salaries with bribes." Those who objected were abused by the Rhee government. Patriotic Koreans did not like it. One Kim Koo, who was particularly vocal, was assassinated. Rhee denied any part in the murder. However, the killer, Lieutenant An To-hi, spent only three years in prison for his crime; which appeared strange, considering that lesser political offenses usually received more severe sentences, often death.

With the passage of time and the hardship of the Korean War, the Old Man presented almost a paranoid approach to any one who opposed his views. Dissenters were accused of being Communists. Anyone who disagreed was at least a traitor. Rhee saw that they were treated as such. There were wholesale arrests, harassments, and frequent executions.

However, to those who agreed with him, he was loyal and forgiving; often he did not even bother to check the performance of favorites. There is the case of the National Defense Corps. When the Communists crossed the 38th parallel and invaded South Korea, the National Defense Corps was sent into combat. They fought bravely, but were badly routed. The survivors who wearily found their way south told shocking stories. They had entered battle with insufficient rifles and equipment. There was nothing for them to eat. The resulting investigation exposed a filthy scandal. The commander of the National Defense Corps had personally pocketed the money appropriated for the supplying of the corps. The master-thief was the son-in-law of Syngman Rhee's Minister of Defense.

Incredibly, during all such peculations and tyrannies, the reputation of Rhee grew brighter and brighter in the United States. He was a fighter and anti-Communist, and the less-favorable facts went untold. The Grand Old Man, he was called, the Stalwart Fighter for Freedom, America's pillar of strength in the East.

By the spring of 1952, the majority of the members of the Korean Assembly were opposed to Rhee; and by law, it was the Assembly which elected the president. Therefore, Rhee, who wanted another term in office, proposed that the constitution be amended so that the president would be elected by popular vote. The reason was simple. Rhee was certain his organization could control a popular vote—about seventy-five percent of which came from isolated rural areas. But he could not control the belligerent assemblymen.

When the assemblymen objected, Rhee again accused them of being Communist pawns. He harassed them. Some of the assemblymen (the equivalent to U. S. congressmen) were arrested. Others had their homes ransacked and searched. He kept up this abuse until the Assembly, wearied, gave in and passed the amendment.

When it came to the actual 1952 election, Rhee's opponent, Cho Bong-am, was shot at. Rhee's party toughs assaulted him, the police heckled him. As a candidate for the presidency, he was unable to campaign. He spent the two weeks prior to the elections in hiding. Even so, at the elections, held in open booths, Rhee's men resorted to intimidation to ensure his election.

There was no end to Rhee's arrogance. By the spring of 1953 the United States was trying to complete the armistice to the Korean War. Rhee opposed it. He did not want the war to end because he was determined to control all Korea. He tried everything possible to block the armistice negotiations; and wanted, instead, to march north and take North Korea. The United Nations disagreed, believing that their mission had been accomplished. The Communist aggressors had been pushed out of South Korea; the United Nations did not think it their job to act as a means to expand Rhee's dominion. Rhee sulked as peace negotiations proceeded smoothly. When it appeared that the armistice would be signed with only the question of prisoner exchange to be settled, Rhee pulled the rug out from under the United Nations. On June 18th, independently and without consulting the United Nations, Rhee released North Korean prisoners. He freed 26,000 prisoners of war to roam across South Korea. These were men who were to be screened by a neutral commission to see if they desired to be repatriated to North Korea.

The Communists at Panmunjom promptly broke off the negotiations. The war continued, and thousands of Americans needlessly were killed.

Finally the armistice was signed—despite Rhee's objection—and the reconstruction of Korea began. Millions of American dollars (eventually 2½ billion) went into establishing factories and businesses, most of which were being run by close friends of Syngman Rhee, most of whom grew rich.

Corruption tainted almost everything in Korea, including the naive Americans. The most widespread example was the black market. It became a disgrace to both the United States and Korea. Thousands of Americans stationed there were familiar with the situation, but little was done to correct it. No U. S. storehouse or PX was safe from pilfering. Stealing and selling of U. S. government supplies was as routine as eating breakfast. I heard a Korean guard say as American equipment was being unloaded, "I hope they don't bring any more of *those* into the country. The black market's already glutted."

A few years ago the U. S. Army received a shipment of new-type jeeps in Seoul. They were the very latest equipment, and were stored in a U. S. Army compound patrolled by armed guards.

A few months later the U. S. military police made a routine check of automobiles in the streets of Seoul. They found about twenty-five of the new-model jeeps—the ones which were supposed to be locked up in the storehouse. The jeeps had been converted into civilian vehicles and had Korean chauffeurs. Drawing the logical conclusion that the cars had been stolen, the military police impounded them.

The next morning the Korean Foreign Office sent representatives over to the U. S. Embassy to complain about the confiscation of the jeeps. The majority of the stolen and disfigured automobiles were now the private property of high Korean officials, including members of Syngman Rhee's cabinet. They wanted their stolen jeeps back regardless of origin.

Over the objection of the U. S. Army, the Embassy bowed before the recriminations of the Korean Foreign Office. As a matter of political expedience, the army was ordered to return the cars to the Koreans who had stolen them. The Embassy did not want to displease The Old Man. And that was that.

One army major told me, "Any Korean who doesn't steal from us is crazy."

By 1955, Syngman Rhee's anti-Communist tirades and threats kept American representatives completely in line, and squeezed from them most of the things he wanted. Black market, intimidation, political chicanery, and corruption were passively overlooked by U. S. officials. In August of that year Rhee increased taxation on foreign businessmen in Korea. It was a harsh law, and Rhee made it retroactive. In the ensuing uproar, the American Embassy attempted to act as mediator. Rhee raged; and even though he gave in on the retroactive provision, he made the Ambassador the whipping-boy. Ambassador Lacy, who had attempted to reason with Rhee, was recalled.

Although a free press was written into the law, in practice there was almost none as far as criticism was concerned. When the Taegu *Mail* attacked Rhee's administration, goons showed up at the paper and wrecked the plant.

The more powerful Rhee grew, the more megalomaniacal he became. During the 1956 elections, when the votes were being counted, the lights went out in the counting stations. Ballot boxes mysteriously disappeared. Rhee's popularity had dwindled so much with the people that he felt fraud was necessary, even though his opponent was a dead man—having died before the election. Nevertheless, the dead man got a sizable vote.

Despite Rhee's efforts, public indignation was so high that the opposition vice-presidential nominee won. But it did not mean that Mr. Chang would be an effective vice-president. The Rhee regime took care of that. In September, Chang was shot at by a Rhee supporter. The vice-president went into seclusion, with armed guards about his house. Since the guards were supplied by the administration, it was a question as to whether they were there to prevent entrance to or exit from the vice-president's home.

During the next four years the Korean people became more and more restless. Rhee sensed the growing discontent, and a few months prior to the 1960 elections, he took steps to control it. He had introduced into the assembly a new set of laws labelled "anti-Communist." Many violations of these were punishable by death. Since anything that opposed Rhee was considered Communistic, it was clear that Rhee was preparing to rig the forthcoming election.* When opposition assemblymen objected to the proposed bills, they were physically carried out of the Assembly and locked up. During their absence, the new laws were passed.

Any observer who had asked questions in Korea knew that for ten years the freedom-loving Koreans were chafing under the Hitler-methods used by the Rhee regime. Even way back in 1952, his re-election had been accomplished by unsavory methods. By 1958 the Korean police state had become so harsh and oppressive that no one was free from political arrest and physical assault.

I briefly visited Korea at this time. Every Korean I spoke to—most of them professors, students, and newspapermen

---

* It was just about this time that a patriotic American organization (Freedoms Foundation), awarded Rhee the Freedoms Medal. Similar awards went to Chiang Kai-shek and Ngo Dhin Diem!

—told me that Rhee's party had to be thrown out; that the people could not take the oppression much longer. "But he is a tyrant," they said, "only because America backs up whatever he pleases."

The 1960 elections were of the same crooked ilk as past ones. People who worked against Rhee's re-election frequently were beaten up. Opposition campaign workers were put in jail. People were threatened that their balloting would be observed by the Anti-Communist Youth Corps.

Election day 1960 seethed with violence. However, there was no problem in Rhee's re-election. The other candidate again had died before the election. It was the second time that Rhee had run against a dead man. But when the much-admired Vice-President John Chang was overwhelmingly defeated by Rhee's unpopular candidate—the Korean nation exploded. They were sure that the ballot counting had been fraudulent—which later proved true. There had been wholesale stuffing of the boxes (and emptying of the boxes, too). Forty per cent of the Rhee ticket votes were phonies.

The people had had enough. Young men began to riot. When the body of a student killed and disfigured by police was found in the bay, wholesale indignation welled over. Demonstrations burst out all over Korea. Rhee blamed the disorder on the Communists; they had plotted all the discontent, he said.

The student demonstrations touched off the long-pent-up misery. Protest meetings, the sacking of police stations, the burning of government offices took place in most large communities. Police used tear gas, in some cases they shot into the mobs with rifles. But the nation's anger at last was in charge.

It was at this time that the Korean people threw Rhee and his gang out of power. It was then—after the Koreans with bare hands had toppled the tyrant—that America finally censured him. Our action was a decade too late. We had put him in power and had given him what he needed to stay there.

The Koreans had been subjected to thirteen years of oppression; and finally they flushed themselves of it. The young people, alone, unarmed, accomplished the cleansing —even though many were killed and wounded in the effort. This patriotism we understand and applaud. But what we do not comprehend is the gullibility, the unending timorousness, and the long suppression of news of Korea by the United States. The excuse offered by our diplomats is that we could not meddle in Korea's internal affairs. Such rationalizing is buncombe. We supported Korea with the blood of our soldiers and with more gold from our treasury than went to any other nation. We had a right to meddle. But because Rhee was a staunch anti-Communist (one of the few such associates we had) we grovelled and quaked before his demands, his false arguments, and his violent tempers. In their ignorance of the facts, our officials believed him simply because he was the Great Rhee.

Public statements by U. S. officials and praise by U. S. editorials at home almost completely distorted the true image of the Old Man.

History shows that Rhee was a practical politician; when hard-pressed he could bend. We were his sole support. Why, assuming he was needed at all, did we not bring pressure to bear upon him to clean house and to institute the democratic processes he himself had proposed?

In this America failed.

All that was needed was facts, courage, and common sense. We flubbed all three. We did not know what was happening. Just as we did not know what was happening in our other failures, in Laos, China, Turkey, Cuba, Chile, Bolivia, Indonesia, Vietnam, and in Iran and Iraq.

5

The Boomerang in the Foreign Student Program

OLD MEN are perhaps the most polished diplomats, but youth changes the world. It was students who finally got rid of the oppressive Syngman Rhee in Korea. In harried and corrupt Cuba, men in their early twenties (many of whom our diplomats didn't know existed) formed the backbone of the revolution that defeated Batista. When Vice-President Nixon was stoned and spat on in South America, the stones and spittle came from the hands and mouths of angry college men.

In Japan, students fighting for what they thought was democracy sparked the riots which prevented President Eisenhower from visiting Tokyo. Turkey's corrupt prime minister, supported by American diplomacy and money, finally was ousted by teenagers. The successful revolt in Indonesia was led by youths not long out of school.

The fact that almost all of America's recent political setbacks throughout the world in recent times has largely been influenced by the wrath and energy of students, brings one to an unavoidable conclusion: United States officials pay too much attention to the old, the status-quo leaders of foreign countries; and they are ill-informed and disinterested about what the younger generation is dreaming and doing. Here again lack of knowledge (not lack of money or good will) is defeating us.

The Communists have been more realistic. They have studied the aspirations and possibilities of the youth movements, and have exploited them to the fullest. Throughout Cambodia, Laos, Vietnam, Burma, Thailand, and Indonesia, hard-core Communists for years have been moving through the land, visiting the little towns. There they have made friends with local mayors; and through them they have identified the brightest and most restless young men of the area. These youngsters from the rural sections —often illiterate—are then offered generous scholarships to schools in China and Russia.

In Thailand, I spoke to two students who said they had gone to the Red People's College in Yunnan Province. They told me that it was the practice to enroll one candidate at the start from each province; later to enroll one young man from each country; and then one from each village. The goal was that every jungle hamlet of fifty families or more throughout Southeast Asia would have at least one graduate from the People's College.

Students from each country are housed in large barracks with others from their homeland. All the instruction is in their own language and there are churches of their preference—Buddhist, Animist, Mohammedan. The priests are of the same nationality as the students.

School lasts eighteen months and the student can take subjects in which he has the most interest. There are short daily discussions on politics. After eighteen months, some of this sticks, and a Communist sympathizer has been created.

My informants told me there were 38,000 students enrolled in Red Schools in Yunnan. Whenever possible the Communists pick the sons or the relatives of the village headman as their students. Later they become party members and organizers. They move from community to community, talking to the elders. It is important to note that it is not a Russian or a Chinese who is doing the persuading. It is a native among his own countrymen. The job of the Russians or Chinese is to train a small efficient cadre, made up of young men wherever possible. The system of working through the chiefs and their relatives is successful.

In May 1960, in Java's provincial election, the Indonesian Communists won 7,500,000 more votes than any other party. Bung Kasimin, a twenty-seven-year-old bellhop in a small hotel, according to the N. Y. Times, explained the situation as follows: "When voting time comes, my village chief tells me how to vote. . . . He tells me to vote Communist."

Bung Kasimin did not know who Khrushchev was, or who the head of the Communist party in Indonesia was. To him his village chief was the chief politician of Asia.

And the young people going to the Communist schools

are the nieces, the nephews, the sons, daughters, and grandsons of the chief. They are the chiefs, the mayors, the cabinet ministers, the presidents of next week and next year.

What the Communists are doing is a contrast to America's foreign-student program. America has not been able to reach the average young people of foreign lands. We have not tried. The relatively small number of students we bring to the United States usually is composed of children or relatives of foreign VIP's. They come from urban areas which represent a small percentage of the population and where the rich are in power. Fluency in English is virtually a requirement for selection.

Several years ago, I had breakfast with President Magsaysay, of the Philippines. While we were eating, an aide brought him a list of Philippine students nominated for scholarships to the United States at the United States' expense. There were about 400 names on the paper.

President Magsaysay began scanning. Going from one sheet to the next, he scratched out almost half of the names.

"These stupid bastards," he said, laughing, "are relatives of politicians. They have money enough to go to America on their own and many of them couldn't pass the exams anyway. They're the ones who always want everything and cause you the most trouble. Why don't you insist on farm boys from the barrios? That's the backbone of my country."

We often fail to pick the right students. On top of that, we have an uncanny talent for insulting the ones we do invite. A frighteningly large number of foreign students are bewildered and antagonized during their stay in the United States. They seldom get to know us for what we really are.

It is a dismal commentary on our failures to note that in Japan, China, and Germany, many of the leaders who were (and are) most vehemently anti-American, are those who were educated in the United States.

In early 1960, the United States government brought thirty-five Africans and Asians on a "leader grant" to the United States. The purpose was to take young potential civic executives and have them see what America was like. It is a good idea. This group visited the University of Hawaii. I spent some time with these young foreigners, and the majority were fine enthusiastic people. But the significant thing was the sprinkling of "ringers" in the group. A man told me he already had been on two other State Department junkets. The two women from Nationalist China were strange choices. The older was a professional junketeer who had spent more time out of Formosa than she had in it, she said, much of it in America. The other one was a nice young girl, the daughter of a governor. Neither of them knew very much about their own country. Other members of the Afro-Asian group were well aware of the "ringers" and commented caustically.

From Hawaii, the students went to the Mainland of the United States. Several wrote and said they had a wonderful time in Hawaii, commenting particularly on the racial integration and their chance to meet ordinary people. They added, however, that they were disappointed with their trip to the Mainland of the United States. They were particularly disgusted with Washington, D. C.

"Washington officials must have thought we were morons," one student commented. "They briefed us on subjects we had read in our own newspapers months and years ago. We had the impression that the officials were busy men who were stuck with a dull chore in seeing us; and that if they didn't watch their language carefully, they might disclose state secrets."

The students were particularly irked at Senator Hiram Fong, the Senator from Hawaii. He is of Chinese ancestry and they were hoping for a frank discussion on Afro-Asian problems.

"As soon as we entered, he picked up the telephone and called for the USIS. They sent a photographer down and took movies of all of us shaking hands with him. We could see him showing the cinema at his next political rally to prove his friends in Asia and Africa. Then the Senator gave us an inane little lecture which indicated he didn't know anything about Asia or Africa; and ended up with scolding us and telling us that we must stop persecuting the minorities in our countries especially the Chinese. He spoke as if he were the Senator from China."

Not long ago, it was necessary to have a small number of simple Cambodian expressions translated into English. The U. S. Department of Defense was unable to locate an American to do the job. The University of California, in looking through its extensive files on Far East experts, found that there were only eleven people in the United States at that time available to do this simple translation. All were Cambodians. Ten of them were in the New York City and Washington, D. C. area. The eleventh man, a young Cambodian student, attended a small college near San Diego.

This twenty-year-old Cambodian college man was invited to San Francisco to do the translation project. He stayed at the home of Professor Eugene Burdick of the University of California.

When the Cambodian arrived he was shy, close-mouthed, and rather aloof. But within two hours—after the Burdick children climbed on his lap—his entire personality had changed. He romped with the children (even changing diapers)—although he laughingly insisted that the Cambodian system of having no back in infant's pants was more efficient. He helped in the kitchen with the dishes, volunteering to cook Cambodian meals for the Burdicks; all the while volubly discussing problems of Cambodia and the United States.

It seems that during the time he was at school near San Diego (about a year), he lived in a little room by himself. He had never been asked into an American home. He had never been asked out socially. His day consisted of getting up, going to school and coming home. He was totally without friends because, as a stranger with an accent, he was too shy to initiate friendship.

"You have better schools in America than there are in France," he said, "but there are hundreds of Cambodian students in France and only a tiny handful of them in the

United States. The reason is that we are lonely in America and are treated like strangers who may transmit a foul disease on close contact. In France, people invite us into their homes and treat us at least as equals and often as honored guests.

"Another reason why there are so few Cambodian students in the United States is that it is easy to exchange our native money into francs; but there are all kinds of problems in exchanging it into dollars. If you have a rich relative in government, it is simple. If you are in a medium-class family, and have no influence, it is almost impossible. So, economically, it is difficult to come to the United States.

"Also, if you are a Cambodian who wants to come to the United States on a U. S. governmental scholarship, you must speak English before you are eligible. There probably aren't 500 people in Cambodia who speak English. To be chosen, you have to be a member of the small, rich clique that is embraced by the U. S. Embassy in Pnompenh. That means, of course, it would have been necessary for you and your family to have been shouting at the top of your lungs that you are anti-Communist.

"Only a small number—you can count them on two hands—of students can manage to come to America even if many wanted to.

"America is making a mistake. Asia is in revolution, and soon the ruling aristocracy will be replaced by children of common people. The Communists realize this. No matter how poor a Cambodian is, if he is intelligent and aggressive, the Communists will invite him to Chinese schools."

Once in Singapore I met Indian students recently returned from the United States. They were delighted to have had the opportunity to travel and study; but they said they had been under tension while in America. They never felt completely welcome. One man told how he had gone into a restaurant in central Virginia and been refused service. They informed him they didn't serve Negroes in the same place with white people.

"A few of us wanted to study cotton agriculture," one said, "and so we asked to enter a southern agricultural university. Life there was unbearable. But as soon as the word got around that we were Indians and not Negroes we were afforded normal social privileges. However we were not asked out often, and had the feeling perhaps people were ashamed to be seen with us. We transferred up north and conditions were happier there."

"We got the impression that once we reached the United States and the universities, that the United States government and the Americans believed that their responsibilities for hospitality were over. Then we were on our own."

Another said, "We observed the Americans to be generous and efficient. I only wish we could have gotten to know them."

And so it appears that because of ignorance on our part the important foreign-student program is not working as well as it should. In fact, in many instances it is backfiring on us. And we are told it is a success.

I I
The Culprits

6

Government by
Misinformation

OUR IGNORANCE of the world outside our borders, and our assumption that an anti-Communist stance is all that a chief of state needs to qualify for our support, are errors which compound quickly and work well for our enemies. What has happened already in Cuba, Korea, Turkey, Iraq, and North Vietnam should have taught us bitter lessons. Yet our government—with the tacit approval of the press—seems content to blame all foreign revolutions on Communists; and after one debacle has passed, we proceed as before to help create the climate in which revolution becomes almost inevitable.

In a period of history when the people—especially the young people—in the so-called backward lands are striking for freedom (in a period of revolution against tyranny unparalleled since the eighteenth century), we are assured by our government that our support of oppressive oligarchies in South Vietnam, Laos, Indonesia, Formosa,

Guatemala, Jordan, Iran, and Nicaragua is constructive and successful. Yet in each of those countries revolt has already shown its violent beginnings; and in each only the United States stands between the people and the overthrow of a corrupt, dictatorial regime. In each, as it already has come in Cuba, Iraq, North Vietnam, Turkey and Korea, the upheaval will come full-blown, and hanging happily on to its coattails will be the Communists—almost as though by our invitation.

Why? Who is to blame? The answer is ignorance: ignorance within bureaucratic circles, ignorance in Congress, caused partly by bureaucratic cover-up, ignorance in the press, ignorance in the American public. The question of who is to blame has many answers. First consider the executive branch of the federal government. Its methods of making decisions reveal much.

Let us assume that the President of the United States is about to make a policy decision. His office in the White House probably is quiet, and he wonders what will happen if his decision is wrong. He thinks perhaps of past presidents faced with similar grave problems affecting the survival of the United States. Now, of course, with the advent of nuclear weapons, more than the United States is at issue. Humanity is the stake. The President pushes a button on his desk; and a few moments later gives instructions to an assistant.

Within an hour the wheels of the executive department are in motion. In the sprawling Pentagon, the Joint Chiefs of Staff are meeting. The matter is urgent; the President has requested advice. Two-star generals and admirals dash in and out of the highly guarded conference room, acting as messenger boys for their four-star chiefs. They are bringing in memoranda and despatches from all over the world. Most of them are marked SECRET or TOP SECRET.

Across the river in the new State Department Building, high civilian officials also are moving in response to the President's request. Perhaps grouped around a table, they are trying to hammer out a recommendation; and much of it will be based on advice received from American ambassadors and their staffs around the globe. This table is also cluttered with SECRET and TOP SECRET papers.

The National Security Council is having a conference under the same conditions; and so is the Central Intelligence Agency. The cream of America's strategic, diplomatic and political brains are working to "get the world picture"—before making a recommendation. They are dependent on information gathered by vast intelligence-gathering systems.

The decision, then, which the President is about to make (and likewise decisions which will be required at lower levels) will be built upon the observations and estimates submitted by American representatives in foreign posts. Who are they?

They are ambassadors, generals, admirals, as well as lesser men. They compose the total overseas membership of the Foreign Service, ICA, USIS, Central Intelligence Agency, and Army, Navy, Air Force and Marine Corps. Their job is to know what is happening in foreign countries. The titles they carry may imply something else and they may have additional duties, but all of them are charged with finding out the facts, transmitting them through the chain of command and frequently making recommendations to higher authority. Vast numbers of them are charged with no other duty.

Leaving the hypothetical President to his decision, let us make an analysis of the sources of overseas information actually available to the government of the United States. The sources are many, but the most prominent and usable are:

(1) Trusted local officials.

(2) Local (foreign) newspapers, magazines, books, radio broadcasts, etc.

(3) Paid local informers.

(4) Personal observations of the nation by U. S. representatives—observations based on intimate knowledge of the people, their culture, language, emotional patterns, etc.

(5) American journalists.

Are these sources of information adequate? Can they be trusted as a basis for forming U. S. foreign policy? It is worthwhile to look at them separately.

1. *Trusted Local Officials*

The opinions and estimates of our ambassadors, generals, and admirals are, in practice, more influenced by local officials than by any other source.

One of the most successful of these foreigners, and typical of many in his value as a source of fact, is a popular (with American officials) Chinese general known in his own country as the Grand Eunuch. (This is fact, not fiction.) He is a big, jolly fellow who was graduated from an American university, speaks our idiom beautifully, and knows American ways well.

The Grand Eunuch carries several high-sounding political and military titles. His major job, however, is to influence important Americans (and, ipso facto, to manipulate United States public opinion and policy). He is famous as an expert in analyzing American officials. He ferrets out their favorite conversational subjects, their weaknesses—be these women, good food, liquor, sports, or flattery. As soon as possible, the general (or whoever else is assigned to work with the American) is supplying the important Americans' needs. If the American has accomplished something in his life—written a book, received a medal, pulled a successful coup, made a lot of money—this accomplishment will be brought into the conversation frequently, with admiration.

Even the most innocent of enthusiasms is grist to the Grand Eunuch's mill. One American admiral was fond of children. Whenever he came to Taipei, the Grand Eunuch met the plane. And with him was a group of attractive, English-speaking youngsters—each with a small bouquet of flowers.

Another technique involves sly bribes in the form of innocent-looking presents. The official who likes fishing is taken to the place where the trout are biting—and receives a beautiful rod and reel. The bookworm gets an exquisitely bound first edition; the hunter, a shotgun. The scholar is invited to seminars with the best-known acade-micians. During this process, our people are skillfully entangled and obliged.

The wives of Americans are not forgotten in the race to warp our flow of accurate information. The Grand Eunuch takes care of the ladies, too. They are certain to have an intimate tea with Madame Chiang Kai-shek. If they are important enough, they will, at the appropriate moment, receive a bolt of precious silk or brocade; or a painting; or jade. But important or not, the wives get *something*.

And, as is well known, almost every high American offi-cial stationed in Taiwan receives either a suitably en-graved silver service or a medal—or both. The least that comes his way is a beautifully painted scroll of apprecia-tion. That is, if he has been of advantage to the Grand Eunuch's government.

If the American has been nosy and belligerent, if he has asked questions and has been tough; if he has worked 100 per cent for America and not tried to please the foreigners —then he gets nothing. Except, of course, the foreign gov-ernment may request he be recalled on the grounds of "not understanding us." This would, in the eyes of the American's superiors, mark him as a failure; and his chances for promotion become less.

The above example is not unique to China. Bribery and flattery of a sort is applied to Americans in most of the foreign nations of the world. As a result, the naive Americans often end up developing a "real friendship" with ministers and heads of states. The Americans too often trust and believe the small group of foreigners who are their "opposite numbers." It is from these "opposite numbers" that much of our important information comes— the information marked SECRET and TOP SECRET.

Frequently Washington officials feel they must supplement the secret papers received from overseas. They must personally go abroad to "see for themselves." They want to get the feel of a country. What frequently happens to them is an outrage to common sense. They get what is known as "the business." Every foreign minister and agency insists on having the honor of entertaining and briefing the distinguished visitors. The ambassadors and generals stationed overseas advise the visiting American VIP's that they must accept invitations or the natives will lose face. And so the few days "inspecting" are spent in a mad rush of briefings, parties, and dinners, usually interspersed with shopping. Result: the American departs in a state of fatigue and ignorance—but with a happy collection of mementos—a silver cigarette case suitably inscribed by the prime minister, native art, etc. His total time has been spent in two or three official mansions, a couple of briefing rooms, and several stores. He has neither seen nor learned much new about the country except what our own—and what foreign officials, which is often the same thing—want him to. Occasionally there are VIP's such as Senator Mansfield, Congressmen Porter and Lindsay, to name a few, who do superb jobs of investigating an overseas area. They are unusual.

In Korea, a small group of Korean officials who were close to President Syngman Rhee had almost daily social and business associations with members of the American government. These "opposite numbers" went on rounds of cocktail parties together, had dinners together, participated in sports together, and sat across from each other at many conferences. These personable and bright Koreans, in reality, became the official eyes and ears of the American government in Korea. They saw to it that our people were so busy that they had few other sources of information. And since our people spoke no Korean they had few choices of intelligence sources.

When the revolution came in 1960 and Syngman Rhee was turned out of office by his own countrymen, his top officials were thrown in jail. It was then learned, for the first time, that many of them were crooks, grafters, and liars. The proof was there. The officials we had trusted and leaned on had fooled us for thirteen years. So we deserted them in jail and looked for a new batch.

The pattern appears to be a common one. In Chungking in the 1940's there were several excellent U. S. military observers and U. S. foreign service men who went into the field and personally inspected the Communist area. They reported that the Communists were well organized and had a strong military machine. However, Ambassador Patrick Hurley, who got his information by hanging around the Chiangs, the Kungs, and the Soongs, (and backed up by a few "yes men" who were close to him at the Embassy) advised Washington not to believe our few professional observers. They simply did not know what they were talking about, he said. There was little to be feared from the Communists, the Ambassador said; he had his information from sources which were reliable. The acceptance of Hurley's advice may well have been the basic blunder of our entire China policy.

At another time, Ambassador Hurley received from one of his foreign-service career men a secret report on the weaknesses of the Chinese Nationalists. To authenticate the information, Hurley called in H. H. Kung, the brother-in-law of Madame Chiang, read the report out loud to him, and asked his opinion. H. H. Kung said the information was false. As a result, the Ambassador never sent the facts to Washington.

2. *Foreign Newspapers, Magazines, Books, Radio Broadcasts*

The foreign press contains much useful information. That is, of course, if the press is free. However, it is not free in China, Formosa, Indonesia, Cambodia, Algeria, Egypt, Ghana, Iraq, South Africa, Vietnam, several Latin American countries, and many others—not to mention members of the Soviet bloc.

Even so, a skilled analyst can learn a lot from local mass media. That is, if he knows the language and can read the papers. Such is seldom the case with Americans. In the majority of the U. S. embassies and consulates throughout the world (along with all other U. S. governmental agencies) the foreign papers are translated for us by paid foreign translators, usually hired on the spot *on the recommendation of the foreign government.* We, the richest and one of the best-educated nations on earth, are incapable and incompetent to do our own interpreting and translating!

Not all the blunders caused by biased interpreting and slanted translating are big ones. But the small distortions, when added up all over the globe, can accrue into a factor which debilitates our national effectiveness. In 1956, for example, when I was in Bangkok I took the embassy's translations of the Thai newspapers and compared them with translations I had had made by three other independent sources.

One of the editorials (according to the embassy translation) praised the American ambassador for being a careful and thorough man in dealing with the Communist problems. The official version said he studied the Red's activities with patience and diligence.

The three translations I had made (each independently) gave a different story. Actually the Thai editorial said that the ambassador spent most of his time looking for Communists under every chair. The implication clearly was that he was a fool. *The account officially sent to State Department was the erroneous one.*

A USIS man told me he had done the same thing in Indonesia. The U. S. Embassy's Indonesian translators had for several years been changing the meanings of news items in the Indonesian papers just enough to have the Americans believe that everything was coming along all right—when actually the original writings had shown much evidence of restlessness and Communist penetration throughout the country.

A distinguished Korean political scientist—a doctor of philosophy—told me he had written a series of articles in Korean describing and analyzing the political situation in his country. He said that he later read the translations which had been made for the American officials and was surprised to find that these translations had reversed his conclusions.

3. Paid Foreign Informers

I do not have sufficient unclassified evidence on this subject to do more than guess from what is available. It appears reasonable to suspect that if our representatives are given consistently bad information by foreign officials who speak English and who are close "friends," they are given no more reliable intelligence from a commercial cloak-and-dagger foreigner.

4. Personal Observations of the Foreign Country by American Officials

Much U. S. intelligence is accepted as fact because the reporter says "I was there." However, our officials are famous throughout the world for the inaccuracy of their personal observations. This reputation is well-deserved. The most conclusive proof of our blindness is that, today, the world is in revolution; and we are not taking advantage of it. People everywhere want to be independent. Colonialism is a hated word. People rebel from oppression. We, as Americans, share their feeling. Our country, instead of helping dissipate colonialism, often has backed the status-quo governments—the ones which the citizens dislike. One by one the people are overthrowing these governments and *the Communists are claiming the credit.* This is a great tragedy. The Soviets basically are colonials and tyrants; yet, because of our inadequate information and resulting blind policies, the Reds are gaining a reputation for aiding oppressed people. They do not deserve the halo, but the point is, they are wearing it.

If U. S. representatives abroad had been competent in their observations they would have seen that revolution in Cuba was bound to erupt. Yet we continued to back Batista until he was thrown out. Consequently we are hated and the Communists—who did nothing—are gaining credits and footholds.

Our officials in Cuba simply did not have enough information on what was going on. And we American citizens didn't know either.

The Department of State is suddenly rushing to send people to Africa and to spend money there. The aid program to Africa is planned to be larger than to any other area—Asia included. Why so late? Nationalism has been boiling in Africa for the last ten years. But we did nothing in that area until riots, civil war, and Communist penetration awakened us. Russians and Chinese who speak local African dialects already are in Africa. Clearly, the Russians must have had information on the growing importance of Africa long before we did. Why should Russian officials be better informed than ours?

5. *American Journalists as a Source of Information*

Much sound intelligence can be gleaned from observations of expert American foreign correspondents. The tradition, however, is that only if the newspaperman confirms the ambassadors' (or ICA or USIS or U. S. military) reports, will the material be approved as accurate and utilized. For example, when Ernest K. Lindley wrote for *Newsweek* that the ICA and military aid programs in Laos were a success and had saved Laos for the West and that therefore Congressional criticism was old hat, his article was distributed widely by the State Department as though it were proof of success. The recent departure of Laos from the western camp into "neutralism" emphasizes the value of such "proof."

If a newsman writes that America is doing a fine job overseas, he becomes the darling of the bureaucrats; he finds it easy to get space on free junkets. If he is critical, he generally is labeled as "irresponsible," or sometimes officials imply that perhaps he is un-American.

Several years ago in Thailand, a New York *Times* reporter wrote a series of articles saying that the Thai government was so frighteningly corrupt that it was in danger of being overthrown. The U. S. Embassy publicly denied the report. However, the newspaperman was correct and the ambassador was wrong. It was not long after that the Thai administration was thrown out of office because the people were sick and tired of its corruption.

And again, Robert Colgrove, a Scripps Howard reporter, wrote a celebrated exposé of blunders and corruption in Vietnam. The Department of State and the ICA marshaled their strength against Colgrove and at a Congressional hearing tried to discredit not only his facts but also his character.

The State Department witnesses tried to destroy Colgrove's story by picking away at inconsequentials. He escaped by the slenderest margin. However, the events of 1960 have proved that Colgrove was right and the State Department has since been forced to admit the truth of many of his charges—but this was long after "State" had shown a nearly vicious anger at the reporting of derogatory news.

There have been several other Congressional hearings on the aid programs—including some on Indochina—which have brought out far more shocking things than Colgrove wrote about. Colgrove, however, was pilloried because the articles in the Scripps Howard papers were read by several million Americans. They had an influence upon public opinion. Unfortunately, Americans do not read the reports of their Congressional committees, and the press usually neglects them.

I once spent an evening discussing "Information Gathering Activities of Americans Overseas" with a group of experts at Harvard University. Two ex-foreign-service officers attended. They said that our representation is excellent only in big European countries such as England, France, and Germany; but in the smaller nations of Africa,

Asia, and South America we are doing a poor job. American officials do not know what is happening. We get sucked in.

The two ex-foreign-service men added that our individual officials are intelligent and patriotic; but that "the system" prevents them from doing effective work. They explained the "system."

First, it is traditional in the United States government that a man should not be a specialist. Senior members who sit on selection boards generally will promote the man of varied experience and pleasant personality over the knowledgeable, tough-minded specialists. This is true, they said, in all governmental agencies.

There is, therefore, no reward for being a competent and candid area-specialist, especially if the area is a small out-of-the-way country such as Laos or Korea.

Also, the ex-foreign-service men continued, most civil servants prefer stations in the more pleasant posts. For example, living in Europe is comfortable. There is good food, healthy environment, theaters, symphonies, and a culture with which we are familiar.

In contrast, residing in a place like Pnompenh or Vientiane is rugged and unpleasant. There are debilitating factors including malaria, intestinal parasites, and poisonous snakes. The climate is uncomfortable; luxuries and amusements are few.

Why, then, should a career man volunteer to become a specialist in an area which brings him little prestige, promotion, or physical comfort?

Also, the two ex-foreign-service men officers told of

another factor which diminishes the effectiveness of Americans abroad. The foreign nations themselves don't want knowledgeable and vigorous Americans stationed there. Such astute experts recognize the ploys, the grabbings, the intrigues which the natives use on inexperienced "trying-to-please" officials.

During World War II, for example, when an American command was being established in China, a Chinese official told the American commander that now that China had achieved independent status, it was not right for the Chinese to suffer the indignities and insults which previously had been given them by "old China hands." He requested, therefore, that only inexperienced, non-Chinese-speaking Americans be sent to China.

The American commander believed this line completely. China experts were forbidden in the area. Instead a bunch of patriotic ignoramuses (on China) joined the American command. Each was assigned an official Chinese interpreter. And it was no accident that the interpreters were members of Chiang Kai-shek's highly trained secret police.

Once again, U. S. activities involving hundreds of thousands of troops and multibillion-dollar expenditures were run on phony information. Today China, the world's largest nation, is Communist, and we have no diplomatic relations with it whatsoever.

Our foreign-relations business, then, is being run on doubtful facts. We are like a sandlot team sent to play in the World Series. No wonder many of our leaders have been too timid to make difficult decisions. No wonder they have procrastinated, and seem to hope that America's good reputation will somehow pull us through. They have not had accurate information on which to base decisions. Mostly they have had the second-hand rumors, guesses, and propaganda supplied by ill-informed amateurs.

7

Secrecy in Government

THE CULT of government secrecy is growing.*

The practice has become so widespread and routine that, according to testimony given before the House government information sub-committee, more than a million Federal employees are empowered to classify information. This means that one out of every 180 Americans is stamping the word "secret" on papers. Thus our protective machinery has become so bulky it no longer is effective for really classified material; and, instead, it has turned into a monster which often swallows information which should be public knowledge.

Pictures of plush furnishings inside military transport planes, requested by Rep. Daniel J. Flood, were stamped "secret" and then even the Congressman's letter of request was stamped "secret." Rep. Flood said, "It appears to me that this classification is designed to protect bureaucrats from embarrassment and not to protect the military secrets from potential enemies of the country."

* Most of the specific examples in this chapter were gathered and published by the Advancement of Freedom of Information Committee of Sigma Delta Chi, a fraternity of professional journalists. Their campaign for abolishing unnecessary secrecy in government is outstanding.

Obviously it is necessary to keep vital defense and diplomatic information away from potential enemies. Few citizens would dispute this. The guarding of legitimately secret material is important; but it has its own built-in dangers—some of which, if they get out of hand, can damage the nation even more than the loss of legitimately classified information.

The Chicago *Daily News* published on July 2, 1957, that a report on profiteering by foreign suppliers of the United States Military Services and the International Cooperation Administration had been classified and would not be released by the General Accounting Office. According to this newspaper, the lid was clamped on this scandal to prevent its revelation during discussion of Congressional appropriations for defense and foreign aid.

Often the triple-locked drawer of official secrecy becomes a hiding place for public problems which officials are frightened to discuss; or legislation they wish to delay; or scandals they desire to hide. It provides the government with an unethical device for releasing only such public information as is convenient.

Intelligence estimates of the Central Intelligence Agency are of the highest order of secrecy. Yet on November 19, 1956, on the eve of testimony of CIA officials before Congressional Committees on the effectiveness of their activities, the CIA "leaked" to favored newspapers the fact that it had given the White House 24 hours' notice that a British-French-Israeli attack would be launched on Egypt. Had the CIA made an intelligence estimate to the opposite effect, it most certainly would have been regarded as too secret to mention.

The stampede for secrecy started with our development of the atomic bomb. As long as America had a monopoly on this weapon, we could keep order in the world. Our diplomatic demands could be loud and simple. American scientific and technological superiority had made our international relations easy. Complete secrecy on the bomb would guarantee that this pleasant situation continued.

Then came the frightful shock of learning that the Russians also had the bomb. *Who violated our security?*

Other paralyzing blows followed: the revelations of Igor Gouzenko, the Russian code clerk. He told of a tremendous spy ring in America and Canada, a spy ring largely peopled by Americans and Canadians. We were also shocked by the Alger Hiss trial; the Bentley and Chambers testimonies; the convictions of Allen May and Klaus Fuchs; the Korean War; and finally the Russian triumph of Sputnik.

Spies, leaks, traitors, seditioners, subversives seemed to be crawling from under rugs and out of the woodwork. A hysteria panicked bureaucracy. Where could these security violations be coming from? (Still, despite the frantic measures to insure security, almost every embassy, military unit, USIS and ICA establishment overseas—and even CIA —employed foreigners as switchboard operators, receptionists, chauffeurs, servants—and in other positions privy to hearing conversations of governmental executives, of picking up papers, of witnessing the daily tenor of the place, observing the arrival and departures of personages with secret orders, etc.) We began to stamp "secret" on everything.

The Department of the Navy declined permission to Captain George W. Campbell for his story of the sinking during World War II of the cruiser *Indianapolis* to be printed in the *Saturday Evening Post* on the grounds that it would impede recruiting. When the *Saturday Evening Post* finally gained clearance from the Secretary of the Navy, the Navy Personnel Department, in a letter stamped "private communication" threatened censure of Captain Campbell.

The growth of secrecy-mania has resulted in citizens being denied information about the workings of the government whose only purpose is to serve the citizen. The bureaucrat has become a self-styled-sacred person; and the common man is blocked from finding out what the bureaucrats are doing, let alone controlling them.

The Post Office Department denied the *Indianapolis News* information on the names of persons leasing post office buildings in Indiana to the government, the amount of the leases, and the duration.

The problem is how much "right to know" can citizens give up in the name of government (and other public affairs) without stepping uncomfortably close to totalitarianism? If free Americans voluntarily *elect* to reduce their right to know—because an emergency requires it—this, then, is their privilege as members of a free society. But this has not yet occurred. At present we want information, and it is being denied us.

The Department of Defense ruled that only those persons with a "legitimate interest" are entitled to know the location of military bases where liquor is sold by the bottle; the ruling specifically mentioned wholesale liquor-dealers, but it implied that a member of the Women's Christian

Temperance Union would be denied the information on grounds of a lack of "legitimate interest."

In the April 1959 issue of *Progress* Magazine, Senator T. C. Hennings, Jr., wrote that:

"Possibly the most celebrated example of outright suppression of information in recent years is the refusal of the Administration to release the Gaither Report to Congress. This report was submitted to the President by a group of prominent citizens after a lengthy study of national security requirements. It reportedly warned that the United States faces its greatest peril in history. Despite its great importance to the nation as a whole, the Administration refused to reveal the contents of the Gaither Report to either the Congress or the public, apparently because of the great political embarrassment and public excitement which might have prevailed."

There has been much argument over the Gaither Report. Many responsible people believe it was proper to suppress the information from both Congress and the public on the grounds that it was, in effect, research done by a Presidential committee as advice to the President. However, when rumors leaked out that the Committee believed the nation to be in grave peril, many legislators and editors believed that some knowledge of this danger should voluntarily be given Congress. It never was.

A publisher tried for months to obtain a list of 50 top officials in the Pentagon who were serving "on leave with pay." This term means these men were drawing down both their regular salaries from their private employers and also full salaries from the Department of Defense. The publisher was refused this list.

In recent years, secrecy in government has gotten worse. The doctrine of "Executive Privilege" was established by George Washington to maintain the privacy of White House plans, discussions, and correspondence. Such protection is needed by the Chief Executive. But now (1960) the doctrine has been spread by Presidential letter and attorney-general ruling to embrace all executive department activities. These include, of course, State Department, Defense Department, and ICA. Furthermore, most of the Executive Department—the approximately 2,000 active agencies, bureaus, and departments and more than 5,000 advisory bureaus—conducts business in the secrecy of "executive session." As an example of this "iron curtain," the 5,000 advisory bureaus do not even make the minutes of their meetings available for inspection to the citizens who pay the taxes.

Teams of State Department and ICA officials are sent to foreign countries to evaluate the American programs there. These reports, because of "Executive Privilege," are not made available to Congress. How can we know what is happening? Must Congress go overseas? Or must we wait until there is an international explosion before we are cut in?

The practice of "Privileged Information" is another government technique for withholding what often should be public property. In many instances the stamp of "Privileged Information" is used to keep unpleasant or unsavory "secrets" from the people. Lists of Congressmen and their wives and dependents who go on free trips all over the world (and spend counterpart funds which they draw limitlessly from embassies abroad) are almost impossible to get. This is considered "For Official Use Only."

Out of fear that public indignation would put a stop to junkets, the "inspection" trips of almost all public officials and their wives is considered as classified. The officials' fear is well founded. If the public knew about these trips, public opinion would soon put the axe to them. Last year there were over 1,000 VIP's recorded as having "inspections" of Hongkong alone—a place which requires little inspection but which is superb for shopping and sightseeing.

The range of suppression seems endless. The Department of Agriculture denied to the Aberdeen (Miss.) *Examiner* the names of Mississippi farmers who were paid not to plant cotton.

There is so much federal secrecy that even the records of the federal expenditure of tax dollars are *not* open to the inspection of citizens, as are the records of city, county, and state governments throughout the land.

The Dayton *Herald-Journal* was unable to get official financial figures on the Annual National Air Show even though the Air Force, at taxpayer expense, furnished most of the airplanes and pilots.

About 80 billion dollars have been spent on foreign aid. We know how much is spent in general areas; but the way the money is allotted in individual countries is classified. Under this secrecy how can the American people ascertain whether their tax billions are honestly being spent at the terminal points; especially when the history of past expenditures reeks of inefficiency and corruption?

William H. Fitzpatrick, Associate Editor of the *Wall Street Journal*, testified: "If government insists on secrecy, how could the people assemble to discuss the state of the Nation or petition the Government in the interest of their personal lives and fortunes? That must be the ultimate end of growing secrecy.

". . . But an uninformed people must, in the end, become a misinformed people. And a misinformed people, while they may be told that they are safest and happiest in their serfdom to secrecy, are not a free people."

8

Government by
Publicity

OUTSIDE the closed door a guard stopped unauthorized persons from entering. Inside, a Congressional investigating committee impatiently waited to go into action. Puffing pipes and cigarettes, the Congressmen were reading a piece of paper marked CONFIDENTIAL. In the center of the group stood a public-relations expert; he was talking slowly, carefully explaining the confidential paper. It was an instruction sheet telling how to get maximum headlines and publicity from the approaching Congressional investigation.

The expert made clear to committeemen how to terminate each day's session so that it would have the greatest news value, how to squeeze the most newspaper space for a press release, how to handle witnesses so that they don't dissipate the publicity angle the committee might be trying to exploit for that day.*

* The points listed on the confidential instructions are given in Douglass Cater's book, *The Fourth Branch of Government.*

The desire of this committee for publicity is common among governmental circles. Almost every official, from the president down, has been guilty of manipulating and managing the news in the predatory struggle for headlines. Washington officials have plenty of free assistance in their "government by publicity." *There are twice as many governmental public-relations men in Washington as there are journalists.*

In the effort to influence our votes and our opinions, Congressmen—along with most other public servants— often forget that one of their primary functions is to inform the country about the conditions and problems of the nation; and to describe important issues so that we can understand them. It was because of this requirement that the post of "public information officer" (or public affairs officer or press attachés) was established.

However, in practice, public information officers (who speak for the various governmental departments) have become prostituted. They have ceased serving you and me. Instead they have developed into press-agents. Almost all of their energies and talents are spent keeping themselves and their bosses in power, obtaining appropriations, or making the bureau "look good," frequently at the expense of other bureaus. In short, much of our government's energy is squandered in obtaining a pre-determined public opinion. Officials try by selective information releases to have us accept what they believe is proper; as if fearing the decisions we might make on our own if we had all of the truth.

Senators and Congressmen (who are so inclined) seem

to publicize themselves with more vigor and skill than other public servants. Perhaps it is because the floors of the Senate and of the House provide a better national spotlight.

Although he is dead now—and almost forgotten—Senator Joseph McCarthy was a master at manipulating public opinion to gain his own end—which was personal power. He effectively used headlines to frighten people, to strangle the usefulness of officials, and to eliminate anyone who impeded his obsessions.

McCarthy succeeded because he discovered and made full use of a tradition of American journalism—that most newspapermen report the news "straight." This means that if a prominent person says something sensational—even if untrue—the press normally will report the statement exactly as spoken. The substance of the speech will not be challenged; and no discussion of its veracity (or lack of veracity) is given to the reader. The press simply acts as a mirror. Therefore the irrational blatherings of a fool get as much publicity as the studied wisdom of a patriotic genius, if the fool is "news" at the time of his blather. The more violent and impossible the speech, usually the larger the headline and the more space it gets on page one.

When a Congressional investigator or a public official as prominent as McCarthy explodes verbally in public, the press merely describes what has happened. Background material or significance of what has been said is not included. *It is up to the reader* (who cannot ask questions or challenge alleged facts) *to differentiate between truth and falsehood.* The gentlemen of the press maintain this is the citizen's responsibility; even though, generally, you and I are not equipped to carry such a complex burden alone. Apparently they forget that we are depending upon them to supply us with *full* information on events.

When McCarthy, from the floor of the Senate, said he had in his hand a list of 205 card-carrying State Department Communists—we were offered no reason to doubt that he really had such a list. It said so in the papers. If our journalists had asked McCarthy for a look at the names and he had refused, we assumed that the press would expose the faker in headlines.

No such thing happened. McCarthy dramatically said he had the 205 Communists' names written on a piece of paper (which he did not); and the press gave us his speech "straight"—thus compounding the deception.

McCarthy knew this would happen; and it was this well-placed confidence which permitted him to shoot his mouth off for several years—always getting publicity from his accusations and ravings. His speeches were news; and the press built McCarthyism into prominence.

It did more than influence us. When one side of an issue is plastered all over the papers day after day, a dangerous phenomenon can take place: The continuous publishing of a viewpoint unconsciously persuades the government that the viewpoint is true; and that it represents a mandate from the people.

What screams from TV, radio, and press is interpreted as public opinion. Which, of course, it is not.

This, then, in addition to personal aggrandizement, often is the aim of Congressional investigations—the circus-type ones which take place on stage before television, radio, and press. We have permitted them to take place even though the sole legitimate objective of investigation is to get information for effective legislation. Douglass Cater, Washington newsman, in his excellent book, *The Fourth Branch of Government,* brilliantly shows how many Congressional investigations simply are a technique for making and controlling news. Investigations, then, often are entertainment spectaculars created to attract public attention. They are a means of molding national opinion or creating fame for the investigators.

Cater wrote, "The most notable committee investigations are seldom point of fact 'investigations.' They are planned deliberately to move from a preconceived idea to a predetermined conclusion. The skill and resourcefulness of the chairman and sizable staff are pitted against any effort to alter its destined course. Whatever investigating is done takes place well in advance of the public hearing. The hearing is the final act in the drama. Its intent, by the staging of an arresting spectacle, is to attract public attention, to alarm or to allay, to enlighten, or yes, sometimes to obscure."

Cater tells how in some of the sensational investigations the information uncovered by the committee was of no legislative importance, ". . . the chairmen sought to dispense with the formality of a report altogether, each making vague assertions that the public had 'the facts' and could form its own judgments." And further, "reporters who have sat through countless hours of these investigations can vouchsafe how difficult it is for a witness to overcome the enormous publicity advantage of a biased committee."

Of course there are some committees, such as the House Committee on Government Activities, whose hearings are modest, dignified, and scholarly. In its quiet way, this committee has discovered information of enormous importance to America—material which influences United States foreign policy and legislation. Yet—despite the fact that this committee's reports are written in clear, readable English and are unclassified, they hardly get a line in the press; and the public is unaware of the Committee's accomplishments.

Is our ignorance the fault of the press for not bringing the committee to our notice in headlines? Is it the fault of the Congressmen for being dignified, fair, and scholarly —instead of putting on a flamboyant show? Or is it possibly that we only show interest in political vaudeville acts?

Although the Congress probably is particularly effective in "prospering by publicity," almost every other governmental activity, likewise, tries to brain-wash America into accepting their points of view.

During my last few trips to Washington I met many public-information officers, some of them old friends. I asked each the same question, "What project are you working on now? Their replies, boiled down, are significant:

The Air Force: "Missiles belong to the Air Force. We've got to get the Polaris away from the Navy."

The Navy: "Something has to be done to stop the Air Force from deceiving the public on their Minute Man program."

State Department: "We are laying low until we see what happens when Kennedy gets in."

The Army: "The Air Force has all the money and the Army is suffering. We want some of the big dough which the fly-boys are hogging, and often wasting."

The missions which our governmental public relations are trying to accomplish may be ethical and legitimate; and they may not. But they are using psychological tricks to capture you and me into a preconceived opinion. The image they are trying to impress on us is created with slanted press releases, cleverly timed speeches, spectacular exhibits, the "leaking" of favorable bits of news to journalists, and having magazines and television publish praising pieces (laudatory articles or pieces which damage their opponents). This is not-too-honest propaganda. We are being treated as bored customers who are shopping for a deodorant or a new car, not as citizens whose independent opinions mold the destiny of our democracy.

We have almost no assurance whether public information coming from Washington is true or not. Some civil servants dish it out for a dozen different reasons, few of them being to inform the country. Occasionally an official —and John Foster Dulles did this frequently—will irresponsibly use the press (and the public) as a means of testing a proposed policy: Dulles would call a private meeting of favored journalists. Everything he told them was "not for attribution." This means his name could not be used. The resulting newspaper articles would start, "High officials in Washington claim that . . ."

On one occasion Dulles gave out a "not for attribution"

story hinting that the United States might defend Quemoy and Matsu. After it was published and the public's reaction was noted, the White House released a story denying that any such action was being considered for Quemoy and Matsu at this time. Although his name was not on it, Dulles authored the second piece as well as the first. By this process of news chicanery he had found out what he wanted to know about the public's reaction. But he also confused the nation.

In *The Reporter* Magazine, Arthur M. Schlesinger, Jr., wrote: "Washington newspapermen today hardly know whether to believe the Secretary of State, because they do not know if he is speaking to them as reporters or seeking to use them as instruments of psychological warfare. . . . What is the responsibility of a newspaperman when he discovers that some rumored development of policy is really only a psychological warfare trick? Should he print the truth at the risk of wrecking the plans of the Secretary of State? Or should he suppress the truth, betray himself, and deceive the American people?"

A similar device used by Washington for influencing us is the clandestine "leak" to a reporter. Hardly a day goes by that we don't read a news story which contains the phrase, "According to well-informed sources . . ."

This means that someone has given out news which he couldn't do officially and honestly. Perhaps it is against the administration's policy; perhaps it is classified; or perhaps it is such a blatant distortion that the official is ashamed to be associated with it.

Of course it is possible the story is only an exciting

rumor which a reporter picked up in a saloon, and didn't have the time or energy to track down and verify.

The hazy and vague explanation of "according to well-informed sources" is like writing the public an anonymous letter.

The government has been shameless in its efforts to attract our attention to a particular point of view, and in this manner mold public opinion. We often are enmeshed into preconceived opinions by the very people we elect and support—the civil servants who are supposed to be doing what *we* want.

The Air Force told its public-relations officers, according to Cater, that "flooding the public with facts is very helpful. But facts, facts and more facts are quite useless unless they implant logical conclusions. Facts must be convincing, demonstrated, living salesmen of practical benefits. These are the only kind of facts that mold opinion and channel the vibrant attentions of public thinking; always deciding issues in the end, altering military policy as surely as defeat in war—they make public opinion the most powerful tool of all, more powerful than war itself."

The Air Force has always worked hard to practice what it preaches; and by skillful publicity has been amazingly successful in favorably influencing legislation. During the first year of the Korean Conflict, the Air Force was probably the least effective of the four military services. But it managed to get the most effective publicity in the press.*

Then, too, there was so much one-sided publicity and

* An eight-month Summary of Military Public Relations at Nieman Foundation 1950-51.

news-muddying (control of our public opinion) during the Middle East crisis in 1958 that our country enjoyed almost no discussion of national policies—either by Congress or by the public. This was the purpose of the administration. Those who spoke in opposition were scolded—by no less than the Speaker of the House and by President Eisenhower himself; and along with the scolding came the implication that anyone who asked questions or dissented came perilously close to being a traitor.

What is the result of all this? You and I are prisoners of our own government's self-generated publicity. Half the time we don't know what is really going on, and to find out we must apply the torch.

9

The Press

It is unpleasant to have to associate the press with those who are helping to misinform the United States. Yet the foreign correspondents and the local reporters are the first to admit that irregularities take place; and they spend long hours discussing what can be done to correct the situation. (Generally it is publishers and owners who deny that there is much at fault with our free press.) There is a lot wrong. The best way of understanding it is to cite examples.

Several years ago during the war in Indochina, two eminent American photo-journalists wanted to do a motion-picture essay on Vietnamese discussing the subject of Communism. Obtaining an interpreter, they traveled north of Saigon to a rural area. Here they interviewed and made motion pictures of village elders, the local chieftains.

The resulting documentary movie was impressive. It was shown on a nationwide television hook-up, and I found it most convincing.

The film started by showing one of the American photographers sitting in a hut with the Vietnamese interpreter and the village chief. The American asked questions such as, "How are the crops?"

The interpreter repeated the question in Vietnamese. The village chieftain looked into the air, thought for a moment, and slowly replied.

"He says," said the interpreter in English, "that the crops are very bad and that there is much discontent among his people."

Other questions dealt with the subject of politics and the feelings of the people toward the French.

In each instance the interpreter repeated the American's question slowly in Vietnamese; and the village chieftain, apparently not used to being interviewed, always twisted his head around, thought for a few moments, and answered hesitantly.

Almost immediately, the interpreter, in beautiful English, told what the Vietnamese had said: things are bad in the village; the situation was raw with discontent; and the area was a breeding-ground for Communism.

The interpreter was so skillful in explaining the delicate nuances that when the film later was shown in Washington, several people in the Department of State commented on how lucky any embassy was to have such an educated and fluent man on the payroll. The documentary movie was then utilized as an official instructional film for Americans assigned to Vietnam for duty; and also as an example of how a good interpreter should function.

Several months later it happened, by chance, that a visiting Vietnamese was brought in to view the show.

He became excited as he watched. When it was over, he said, "You know, of course, that this is a fraud."

It turned out that the interpreter had in no instance interpreted in English what the village chieftain had said in Vietnamese. Often the interpreter had reversed the old man's meaning. In fact, he sometimes did not even tell the village headman what the Americans had asked. Instead, the interpreter had said in Vietnamese, "Now you do as I tell you, old man, or you will get into trouble. When I stop talking, I want you to look up into the air and think for a moment, and then very slowly count up to ten." When this was over, the interpreter made up his own replies. He told the Americans how conditions in the area were terrible and how the people were ripe for Communism.

What was the final result? Two eminent photo-journalists, both of them reporters of skill, courage, and integrity, made a documentary motion-picture which presented false information. The film was shown to a large audience in America *and was accepted as the truth.* The message of this movie was believed not only by the great numbers of people in the United States, but it was also believed by the nation's official experts.

The erroneous information given to America was discovered only by accident. But suppose the journalists had been in Vietnam *writing* the event instead of capturing it on sound film? In that case, the newspapers (and radio and TV commentators) would have carried a by-lined article along the following lines:

"Bha Ho, South Vietnam, 14 October. The farmers in this rich rice bowl of South Vietnam are ready to become Communists. For the past three days we personally have been talking with many village chieftains who are the leaders of this lush and strategically-placed valley. Again and again we heard their stories of dissatisfaction and poverty. Again and again we heard their threats that if their lot is not improved, they will ask assistance from the Communists up north . . ."

Such a news story would be accepted as an eye-witness account by American journalists. What choice have we? We would never have learned that the interviews with the village chieftains had been accomplished through an interpreter. We would never have doubted the interpreter's honesty or fluency. We would have assumed that the American journalist had taken all the precautions necessary to confirm and authenticate the account.

Unhappily, our blind confidence in the press is misplaced. True, we have some excellent foreign correspondents. Professionals such as Abe Rosenthal, Keyes Beech, Pepper Martin, Robert S. Elegant, Tillman Durdin, Robert Trumbull, to name some, are efficient instruments of journalism. It is these few old pros whose work we can believe. Their efforts stop American reporting from going into a complete tailspin. However, in too many instances our foreign correspondents do not know enough about the culture, history, or language of the country concerned to write a first-class story. Neither do they have the time to sift propaganda from fact or to research the background of events. And when their stories reach our newspapers, they are cut and given headlines by editors who know little, if anything, about foreign news. You and I have no way to check on what we read, and we cannot depend on our government to help us.

P.S.: I told the story of the documentary film on Vietnam to John Broger of the Department of Defense. It is to his everlasting credit that he was able to get hold of this film and exhibit it—along with the true story—to military men all over Asia. This film is unclassified, and I urge that world affairs groups, and other patriotic associations, borrow it from the Department of State and show it at their meetings.

Sometimes the press blames governmental officials for holding back information—and often this accusation is merited. There are many instances, however, when the correspondents have no one to blame but themselves for silent officials.

For several years I was special assistant as well as public-information officer to the Commander-in-Chief, Pacific. In succession I had three dynamic admirals as my bosses, Admiral Radford, Admiral Felix B. Stump, and Admiral Felt. The Commander-in-Chief, Pacific, is the boss of *all* U. S. military activities from the west coast of North and South America throughout the Pacific and Asia—as far as Pakistan. This military command touches, or is involved with, nations possessing approximately one-half of the total world's population. Much important news comes from this area, because it embraces such countries as Red China, Formosa, the Philippines, Korea, Japan, Laos, Cambodia, South Vietnam, Indonesia, Burma, India. Therefore many newspapermen travel there.

A large percentage of them passed through Hawaii and interviewed the Commander-in-Chief, whose headquarters is at Pearl Harbor. Before they came to see the Admiral, I usually advised them of newspaper clippings, magazine articles, and books which would supply background information on recent events in the Far East. However, approximately eighty per cent of the newspapermen would come out to Pearl Harbor without having read the suggested material or anything else. *They would not know enough to ask the Admiral intelligent questions;* and they would commence their interview with queries such as: "Admiral, when do you think that the Communists will attack Formosa?" . . . "Sir, I like to write off-beat things, can you give me a few anecdotes about your command?" . . . "If any of our installations are attacked by the Reds, will we use H-bombs on the Chinese mainland?"

When the Commander-in-Chief heard such talk, he ended the interview as quickly as possible. Even if he were inclined to try to answer the impossible questions, he knew it would be difficult to discuss them intelligently with an uninformed interviewer.

The other twenty per cent of correspondents—the Trumbulls, Beeches, Durdins, Martins, and so on—would already have read the material, plus a lot more. When these old pros interviewed the Admiral, they frequently told him things he had not known; and after five or ten minutes the Old Man realized that here was someone with whom he could have a rational conversation and not be quoted out of context. As a result, he granted a one- or two-hour interview and often wound up by inviting the reporter to lunch or dinner.

I have seen this pattern of journalism all over the world. The few professionals—damned few—who become experts are able to capitalize on significant information when it comes along. It was no accident, then, that Keyes Beech of the *Chicago Daily News* was the only correspondent who emphatically warned us about the revolt in Korea. He had done his homework in endlessly reading the Korean press, and checking the contents by going to Seoul and interviewing Koreans. It was no accident that Bob Elegant, Far East correspondent on *Newsweek,* first broke the story on the Chinese communes. He had spent years learning how to talk, read, and write Chinese; and many tedious months reading the Chinese press and listening to refugees. When he received a significant tip, he knew how to put the pieces together.

But what about the hundreds of lesser correspondents who daily file copy from all parts of the world? From them we receive a mishmosh of hand-out stuff that is jumbled and badly written.

Is it any wonder that foreign news is the least-read major subject in the American newspaper? The average paper devotes only four per cent of its total news space to foreign affairs. Which means that we, the readers, spend approximately three minutes a day glancing at world events.

There are instances, however, when the government shamefully fails to assist the press (thus contributing to the false image we have of events).

In about 1955 an exciting story broke in the papers about a Chinese Red attack on the island of Matsu. A fleet of Communist war junks had attempted to capture Matsu. After a long night battle, the Nationalist defenders had repulsed the enemy. The Communists had lost many ships and men.

About this time I went to Taipei; upon arriving I was met by a swarm of angry American correspondents (I was in the Navy). They said they had received the story of the big sea battle from the Chinese Department of Defense at a press conference. It was an important event, but the Chinese authorities would not let reporters go to Matsu to witness the battle for themselves. The Chinese public-relations officials said that they would keep the press informed.

The newspapermen wanted me to have my admiral intercede in their behalf. I suggested that this was not the admiral's prerogative because the senior American official in Formosa was the ambassador.

One of them said, "We can't get the time of day from the sonuvabitch."

They already had gone to the embassy and asked if the story of the battle were true, and, further, had requested permission to visit Matsu. The embassy had replied with a "No comment." The press was told that the U. S. government could not meddle with the internal affairs of a sovereign country; and that the Chinese Nationalists had the right to put out press releases on any subject they pleased.

The American correspondents were in a difficult position. If the account were authentic and they did *not* cable it home, they might miss an important story. So—without confirmation—they sent a report of the battle to the 2,000 or so newspapers of America. They included in the text "according to Nationalist spokesmen a battle raged last night . . ."

When the newspapers in America ran the piece, the readers saw the bold headlines; but the chances are they did not notice the phrase, "according to Nationalist spokesmen." Even if they did, it meant little. The papers did not tell us that the story was unconfirmed. They did not let us know that the correspondents had been refused permission to witness the event for themselves. They did not tell us that the U. S. Embassy had refused to help.

And so, reading our daily papers, we accepted the battle as a fact.

It so happened that by luck I was able to fly to Matsu. While there I asked the American Army observers about the attempted invasion. They had not heard of it. Finally one of them recalled an incident which had happened a few nights previously. A fisherman had lost his way. By accident he sculled his sampan into a defense area. The sentries saw him and fired a few rounds of twenty-millimeter shells across his bow as a warning. The fisherman turned his sampan and sculled back into the darkness and the open sea. This was all there was to the big-sea battle. But that's not the way we heard it at home.

This brings up an important question. Does the government have any responsibility for keeping the American public informed? In the "Matsu invasion" case, to whom did the U. S. government owe its greater loyalty, to a foreign country or to the citizens of the United States? Does our government have the right to deceive us in the name of international protocol?

Does the press have an obligation to take pains to impress on the reader the fact that second-hand information is just that—unconfirmed and possibly false? Does the press have an obligation, further, to carry headlines which are always representative of the story as a whole, and of its reliability as fact?

This kind of inadequate reporting has happened in Formosa, Korea, and Laos. Can it be that the same poor performances are occurring all over the globe? The evidence indicates that they are. The Associated Press, the night before Batista's flight, filed from Havana a despatch which said that the rebel threat to Havana had "faded in a storm of government firepower," and that government troops "hammered retreating rebel forces around Santa Clara tonight and drove them eastward out of Las Villas province." Actually, Batista was preparing to flee. Castro was the victor.

It is not surprising that the Associated Press had made this mistake. The general tone of the news from Cuba for the previous six years also had been inadequate. The American people (and by inference our government, too) had been in ignorance of the cruelty and oppressiveness with which Batista had been governing the Cubans. I am certain that had we been informed, an indignant American public opinion would have demanded that our support, both material and tacit, be ended.

The only explanation I can offer for our being deceived by our press in Cuba is the fact that many newspapers and radio stations in Cuba were on Batista's payroll. They had no choice but to praise the dictator and write favorable stories about him. These same papers were clients of our wire services and were the sources from which they received much of their news on Cuba.

Today we hear rumblings of corruption, dictatorships, oppression and bad administration from other South American and other Caribbean nations. The Communists are beginning to exploit the situation. These ugly situations don't happen overnight. They require years to develop. Then why haven't we been hearing about them before the explosions took place?

Sometimes the press is subtly corrupted by a foreign government. For example, the *Reader's Digest* received an article about Formosa from a well-known freelance writer. The piece was sent to me for checking. I found it chock-a-block with errors and I could not understand how such an experienced journalist could make so many obvious mistakes. Furthermore, I wondered why the *Digest* had sent the writer to China. He had no background or experience in that area.

Out of curiosity I investigated to find out how the author had managed to make so many factual mistakes. Here is what I discovered:

One of Chiang Kai-shek's public-relations outfits in New York had contacted the author, and had offered to pay all his expenses from New York to Formosa and back if he could get a tentative commitment from a large-circulation magazine.

The *Reader's Digest* had said that they'd be glad to see his story about Formosa after it was completed. On the strength of this the author got a free ride to Taipei. While there, the Chinese Department of Propaganda had "assisted" him with material and interpreters; and the author had written the story the Chinese wanted.

This means, among other things, that U. S. foreign-aid money given to the Nationalists for defense was used to propagandize the United States. The author, having received several thousands of dollars' worth of travel from a foreign government, of course should have registered in Washington as a foreign agent.

Fortunately, in this case, the *Reader's Digest* was careful enough to have the piece checked; and, as a result, the article was not published. But what about the other American journalists who, at other times, were also paid by the Chinese to write stories?

Nationalist China is not the only nation which bribes American writers. This practice is common. Press junkets are used whenever publicity or propaganda is needed. The Belgian government flew a plane-load of writers to the Congo several years ago; and this resulted in a rash of articles praising the Belgians for their enlightened administration of the Congo. How do these accounts jibe with the

events of the Congo for 1960? There are few foreign nations who in their struggle for favorable publicity (propaganda) don't offer gratis trips and expenses.

The majority of our reporters and writers are honest
men; but when a nation or organization transports them
as VIP's—especially if they are second-stringers who usually
couldn't make a luxury trip under any other circumstances
—the chances are that some propaganda will end up in the
American press. This is the reason why quality publications discourage their staff members from taking free
junkets. If the area is newsworthy, and commercial planes
fly there, then it is worth paying the reporter's expenses.

Sometimes the press, out of a feeling of patriotism, does
not report to us what is happening.

At the beginning of the Korean War, American forces
—both military and diplomatic—were in a jangle of confusion. The performance of Army troops and Air Force
planes, during the first few months, was something which
is unpleasant to discuss. After Pearl Harbor both of the
commanding officers were court-marshaled for being taken
by surprise. But their troops and crews were well-trained,
and after the initial shock performed with skill and efficiency. In Korea the troops were not well-trained. They
were soft from occupation duty. Even their equipment was
in poor condition. Things were so bad that, in my opinion,
generals should have been court-marshaled.

We know that the Armed Forces voluntarily would
not tell us about such scandalous occurrences. However,

the American journalists, who witnessed everything, didn't tell us either.

In their estimation, it would have been bad for the United States at that time to have learned about untrained troops, lack of rifles, lack of air support for ground troops, bombing of our own people, and administrative chaos in civilian agencies. Whether the press had the right to withhold this information from America has been argued back and forth. To me the decision showed bad judgment; especially as our shortcomings were no secret to the Communists.

There was such an information paralysis during the early part of the Korean War that even General MacArthur did not have adequate intelligence. For example, the U. S. Marine Corps Intelligence tried to tell General MacArthur that the Chinese would invade from north of the Yalu, that Communist troops were mobilizing in that area. MacArthur's own staff members advised him not to believe this. The ensuing disaster is well remembered.

On October 26 the Korean 6th Division informed U. S. headquarters that Chinese troops were attacking them near the Yalu River. These reports were not believed. On October 27 and October 28 the Chinese assaulted four other Korean Divisions. Then the Chinese hit U. S. troops. It was not until almost two weeks later, on November 6, that MacArthur admitted that the Chinese had entered the war. The Chinese and the Russians knew what was happening, but American citizens were denied the information. They were denied it by their government and their press, both of whom knew the truth.

What has become of the fourth estate? Are we to accept the statement of a wire service chief that because subscribers don't want much foreign news his agency need not cover and report it? Are we to agree with the editor who says he can't devote much space to foreign news because his readers prefer the comics? Are we to merely laugh when told by a researcher in the field that anyone living in Texas and wishing to know about the rest of his own country, much less the overseas world, would do better to read the *Toronto Star* than any daily in Texas?

What has become of the original concept of journalism as a profession rather than as an industry?

III
What's to Be Done

10

Specifics at a
National Level

WHAT'S to be done about it?

Our great national failing is our lack of information. Our officials—including the President, the State Department, the Department of Defense, and Congress, frequently have made decisions from ignorance and misinformation. The public has been operating on even less—often on hearsay and propaganda, double-muddied by officials and by the press.

What follows, then, are:

1. Some specific suggestions for assisting both United States officials and citizens in becoming knowledgeable about our world struggle for survival.

2. Some methods of improving the flow of news—both good and bad—so that American public opinion can be based on facts, not propaganda and biased ballyhoo.

3. A blueprint for future action for citizens who, in their everyday lives—from their homes and offices, their

factories and fields—want to participate in the control of the fate of the nation.

One of the first and most urgent specifics awaits the action of the President. One of the most effective actions he could take would be to initiate a program that would ensure the collection of accurate information overseas, and that it is made available to the nation. Currently, many members of Congress are openly skeptical of the "facts" they receive from the State Department, ICA, and the Department of Defense. The Congressional Record is full of Congressional doubts concerning the information received from the Executive Department.

There appeared to be a fear, throughout the Executive Branch, to tell anyone anything—except to report success. (It is a philosophy of information which perhaps was best expressed in a statement attributed to Admiral Ernest King during World War II. When asked how detailed should be the battle reports released to the public, he is reputed to have said, "Don't tell them anything. When it's over just tell them who won.")

For example, it is the custom to send "evaluation teams" overseas to measure how well or poorly our foreign policy programs are working. If failures are uncovered, the teams report on the causes.

Yet such evaluation reports frequently have been classified as secret. Even Congress normally could not see them, especially if the report indicated danger or failure.

The reports, in some form, should be made available to Congress. How can Congress make wise laws and appropriate money for foreign operations if it is denied pertinent information by the Executive Branch?

President Kennedy has announced that during the course of each year he will make a number of reports to the nation on the state of its affairs. It is to be hoped that he will follow his own lead and spell out bad news as well as good. We cannot function as citizens if we remain in ignorance of our national problems.

The President should assume that his fellow countrymen are tough-minded and patriotic. We will not become timorous or demoralized if told the truth about our blunders, failures, and defeats. Quite the contrary, we will respond with strength and intelligence. But first we must have the truth.

A Permanent Corps of International Experts

Another of the President's key problems is replacing our amateur government officials with professionals. Accurate information (and the decisions which result) can come only from highly trained, dedicated public servants.

For every country in the world we must have a supply of international specialists. They must know the dialects, the terrain, the commerce, the flora and fauna. They must be efficiently familiar with every ethnic group and tribe; and be able to predict with reasonable certainty how these groups and tribes will react to different physical, intellectual, and political pressures. They must know the emotional and mental patterns of all strata of the country's society; and have the ability to negotiate with confidence and success in jungle huts as well as grand palaces.

We do not have many such professionals available; we will have to train them from scratch. They form the blood and guts of the major weapon of today's war of propaganda, politics, and economics; and we must create this weapon from almost nothing—with at least the vigor with which we created the first atomic bomb. We must start with young men and women who are tough, pliable, and bold.

At this critical moment in our history we have effective plans for procuring selected, upper-level public servants only in the area of the military. The Navy, for example, has a highly successful officer-procurement program whereby it underwrites a portion of the costs of college education for qualified young men. In exchange, the potential officers agree to include in their curricula a minimum number of courses specifically designed to train them for naval service; and they contract to remain in the Navy for at least three years after graduation. They may then resign, and return to civilian life. Or, they can make the Navy their career.

A similar system could be applied to the development of a Foreign Specialist Corps. Candidates for this program would be selected from among those applicants among the high school seniors whose aptitudes and scholastic records meet specified requirements (there is a powerful appeal as well as a practical usefulness in an elite based on attainment). The government would pay each accepted student's way through two years of college, and during their college years the selected young people would be required to take a number of courses to train them for their future government service. They would be given as much choice as is practicable in selecting their geographical areas of specialization and in choosing the college which they will attend —within limits of scholastic standing and the availability of courses concerning the countries in which the student is specializing. During summer vacations, student specialists would be sent overseas for six weeks of practical work. Their status and pay would be equivalent to that of a midshipman at the Naval Academy. Their duties would include on-the-spot language training plus lower-level jobs in a U. S. government agency.

After graduation, the specialists would receive another six months of concentrated instruction abroad. During this time they would receive heavy doses of the foreign-language training and would travel throughout the country so that they see every inch of it at the common man's level.

Their training completed, specialists would be obliged to serve abroad for three years. They would work at a job where their background could best be utilized; and where they are most needed. The specialist might act as embassy interpreter; or he might supervise a construction project, be a political analyst, or any of the other thousand tasks which need doing.

The three-year overseas tour would take the place of military duty (although if the specialist elected to serve abroad as a member of a military service he could do so). Upon expiration of the three years, the specialist may resign and return home. Of course he would be a member of the Overseas Reserve Corps (or whatever the corps is titled) and, in time of emergency, could be called back to active duty—just as military reservists can be recalled. Periodically, if he desires, he would be sent overseas for a month at government expense—perhaps every two years, so that he can maintain his skill at the language.

He may make government a career. If only ten percent did this, it would not be too many years before all branches of the government had a skilled hard-core of able young people who would be experts in foreign fields. They should get pay rewards for additional skills, such as language proficiency.

The ninety percent who leave government service and return to civil life would not be wasted. The money spent on their schooling would be well invested. Their knowledge of international matters would enrich the entire United States. Trained specialists would flow into industry, the press, the universities. Gradually our international businesses, our foreign-correspondent corps, our schools would be able to do their jobs with knowledge and efficiency. In time, the entire level of our nation's proficiency in foreign affairs would rise.

Utilizing Wasted Manpower and Talent

The large majority of young men summoned to draft headquarters fail their physical examination for military service. They are rejected; and the task of defending the United States is left to the minority who are lucky enough to be completely healthy.

Sometimes as high as seventy percent of the most vigorous age group in our society (the "most powerful nation on earth," we call ourselves) is prevented from serving their country because they are considered unfit for violent combat. Yet our nation is endangered by a nonviolent battle—the Cold War—that is as deadly as combat and more difficult to wage. In this type of struggle (and we can lose it without a shot being fired) the physical rejects could be capable soldiers.

There are hundreds of thousands of tasks all over the world which today are being bungled or not being done at all. Some jobs are being let to contractors (a frequent source of corruption and graft), some are worked at by a pampered and expensive civil service, demanding commissaries, cars, post exchanges, first-class transportation, and social standing overseas far above their normal station. Countless jobs are being performed by foreigners, many of whom are in sensitive positions and are security hazards.

The excuse generally given for the employment of foreigners, of a pampered civil service, and of profiteering contractors to wage the cold war is "What else can we do? If we don't use these methods we can't get the job done at all."

Congress has authorized the University of Colorado to study the problem of the wasted manpower of youth, and a report will be ready soon. Meanwhile, what follows suggests some of the lines we might pursue in our efforts to solve it. We can draw on all the millions of young men eligible for the draft, including those who fail their military service physical examinations. Those unfit for combat owe the nation the same sacrifice as do the more rugged. Let us select from the entire pool of youth those whose aptitudes particularly suit the needs of what might be called the United States Strategic Service Corps. It would be comparable to the military in training, discipline, regulations, pay, and length of service. The major difference would be in duty assignment. Instead of standing by to fight in combat, Strategic Servicemen (and women) would be fighting every day in the Cold War.

The money saved would be breathtaking. The ability to select from the *entire* mass of our youth those best fitted for strategic service in every area of international effort would increase efficiency and build a reservoir of knowledge now lacking. A hint of how this would work can be illustrated by observing Okinawa in 1957. During that year the Americans stationed there consisted of Civilians, Army, Air Force, and Marine Corps. For all groups, *except the Marines,* Okinawa was a luxury post. There were comfortable quarters. Families were brought over. Servants were cheap. Recreation was plentiful. Duties were easy. The popularity of the post is indicated by the fact that in the Army it had the highest re-enlistment rate of any station in the world.

The Marines were not permitted to bring their families. They were in Okinawa as a combat unit, ready to fight any place in Asia. They lived in barracks in a relatively undesirable but militarily important area of the island. Their training schedule was far more rigorous than that of any other service. Because it was a duty post for them, not a "home away from home," it cost considerably less to maintain a Marine in Okinawa than it did a civilian or an Army or Air Force man. Yet, their standards of performance were as high, if not higher, than that of other Americans: *and the Marines enjoyed it.* Their re-enlistment rate was even higher than that of the comfortable Army. This is a principle which should be applied to a United States Strategic Service Corps.

The example of the Navy's Construction Battalions, the famed Sea Bees of World War II, applies perhaps even better. It was an outfit of "old men," of physical rejects in many cases. Yet their story is one of the glories of the war.

The tasks the United States Strategic Service Corps could accomplish throughout the world are innumerable. They could construct the much-needed housing in Korea, the roads in Thailand, the electrical lines in the Philippines, the thousands of medical dispensaries required all over Africa and Asia.

In most cases where foreigners are employed, in the United States missions, Strategic Service personnel could take over. This could well include jobs as chauffeurs, telephone operators, truck drivers, PX clerks, and on up the scale. Then, instead of having our Foreign Service, ICA, USIS, and Military Assistance Groups infested with personnel whose loyalty lies with a foreign country (and one of the best means of espionage available to our enemies), we could have loyal, well-trained, English-speaking Americans.

Our young Americans are not originally equipped to do such work any more than newly drafted men are capable of their military duties. They have to be trained, just as military draftees are trained.

Such a corps of lower-echelon overseas workers would provide another and less tangible value. Today the foreigners, especially the nations of Asia and Africa, see mainly those Americans who try to live at an almost ambassadorial level. Stenographers put on the airs of a society queen. Almost all the more menial duties are performed by natives, a fact which helps create the picture of Americans as Caucasian colonials. Nothing would destroy this undesirable reputation so much as seeing Americans who are not ashamed to work with their hands. Although we are proud of our capacity and willingness to do this at home, for some reason when overseas we avoid it ostentatiously.

It is also proposed that these young people (and there is no reason why women cannot be brought into the Strategic Service Corps) be housed overseas in barracks in a quasimilitary set-up, with military discipline. They should go abroad without dependents—*exactly as though the nation were on a wartime status,* because we are at war.

Having a battalion of American civil servants building native housing with their own hands, creating irrigation in deserts, rigging electrical equipment, driving cars, or as menials, bargaining for fish in the market place, would have a great psychological impact.

There will be obstacles to surmount in organizing a Strategic Service Corps, and there will be objections from many sides. But consider its possibilities:

(1) It will make available the services and talents of a majority of the nation's youth—a precious strength that today is being wasted—in our area of greatest national need.

(2) It will increase the efficiency of countless operations all over the world.

(3) It will diminish the cost of our overseas programs.

(4) It will reduce the espionage opportunities open to our enemies.

(5) It will build up the health and prestige and dignity of the majority of our young people—the majority who today are rejected from military service.

(6) It will embellish the American image overseas; and will increase our prestige.

(7) It can reduce the corruption and graft which has plagued and debilitated almost every foreign-aid program we have attempted.

(8) Over the years, it will create a reservoir of citizens who have had training, experience, and first-hand knowledge of the world outside our borders and of the problems we must face there.

Is it not worth a try?

A Foreign Student Program

It is important that we know foreign lands and people, but it is also necessary that the foreigners know and understand us. Such education abroad can best be effected by the foreigners themselves.

Working from the obvious fact that the youth of the emerging nations of Africa and Asia are rapidly assuming leadership there, we must set up a massive yet selective program designed to bring students from these lands to be educated in the United States. We should have large numbers of students from every country in the world. The program must be designed to help the youth of all classes of society and occupation. A knowledge of English and social position should no longer be requirements for obtaining a scholarship.

Strides have been made in this area by organizations such as the American Field Service, and the Experiment in International Living. This type of program needs to be multiplied and expanded many times before national requirements can be filled.

The subject of student exchange is so complex and involves so many schools and agencies that the President immediately should appoint a committee to:

(a) Set up the standards required for different classes of foreign students.

(b) Designate the different categories of students we will invite. Some may be illiterate but skilled in manual crafts. Some may be at the high-school level, some college.

(c) Arrange to bring the students to America for six months or a year before the school starts—in order that they may learn English.

(d) Ensure special instruction which will teach them how to carry out their skills *with the equipment and conditions in their own country*. Today there are thousands of foreign graduate students in America who do not wish to go home because what they have studied does not apply to the circumstances at home.

(e) Determine the most urgent needs of the various foreign countries, so that the most necessary skills can be taught first.

(f) Arrange a social program which will make the foreign students feel at home in America. There are excellent programs already in action in several cities (notably Philadelphia) which would serve as models. Some churches do well in bringing together foreign students and local young people of common interests. In any case, intensified local efforts to bring foreign students into the life of the community are badly needed and would pay off in future understanding at the highest level.

(g) Set up the machinery to find the right students abroad. (For example, in Buddhist countries we could ask the assistance of the priests, who traditionally are in charge of education.)

(h) Draw up legislation which would reimburse American schools for the costs to them of foreign students.

(i) Draw up legislation providing for housing the foreign students. They should have the opportunity to live in private homes.

(j) Arrange a program whereby American students, in exchange, can study in undeveloped foreign countries under government auspices or at least get practical experience there. M.I.T. at present sends engineering students to work in Africa for the summer. Harvard is planning a working seminar in Nigeria. For every opening in programs such as those at M.I.T. and Harvard there are hundreds of applicants. Our young people patently recognize the challenge and are responding to it. However, a vast extension must take place if the response is not to be wasted.

If we are sensible and thoughtful, and if we offer foreign students what they truly need, we can have an unlimited number of young foreigners from every nation in the world enthusiastically in favor of America.

By no coincidence at all, what most young people all over the world want, America provides. America permits a liberal environment, a fluid society, the freedom to wear one's hair long or short, to listen to cool jazz or classical music, to stand up and speak, to protest, to agitate, to stretch the intellectual and social muscles. In Russia and China and in their satellites this is impossible.

Visitors to Russia and Communist China and the satellites report that students there ape American ways. One of the most sought-after and precious things among Russian students is an American jazz record. By what accident, then, do students around the world think that the Communist bloc offers more enthusiasm and a broader outlet for them than we?

Somehow we must multiply our efforts to bring our jazz, our eccentricities, our literature, our adventure, our enthusiasm, our zeal for experimentation to the young people overseas who, not too long hence, will be the ministers of state. But we do not. Aside from the all too few students who take advantage of the American Field Service and Experiment in International Living programs, the only Americans the foreigners see in their own countries are a bunch of middle-aged American military and diplomatic people dealing with middle-aged diplomatic and military people in their country; they see protocol, comfortable living patterns, and status quo. The exciting prospect of bringing our youth and its enthusiasm to the youth of these countries must be explored much further. The student-exchange program must be expanded.

The 4-H Clubs of America have set another successful example. In a remote spot in the Philippines I met two 4-H-ers participating in a native dance. Afterward, they put on a jitterbug demonstration in which the Filipinos soon joined. The 4-H-ers ate rice and adobo, and slept on the floor of a nipa hut. The next day the Filipino youngsters and the American youngsters exchanged agricultural information.

One of the Filipinos said, "This is what both our countries need. But the government has to start it. We don't have the money to travel on our own."

He added, "And you know, there are a thousand artesian-well rigs in storehouses in Manila. The Philippines are desperate for drinking water; but we don't have the engineers to install the rigs. I'll bet that if a couple of hundred American engineering students came here for the summer, between us and them we could get those wells going. And if a number of us went to American schools every year, and in return were obliged to work for the government for equal time—then in the future we could handle these problems for ourselves."

What the Press Can Do

A paper cannot be well-edited for foreign news if the staff is ill-informed on world events. I suggest that papers subscribe to the American Universities Field Staff Reports. In my opinion, they represent the most distinguished reporting-in-depth there is on world affairs. Also, I recommend subscribing to the airmail editions of *The Economist, The New York Times,* and *The Asahi Evening News.*

Beyond that, we need newspapers managed by people who realize the importance of what they are doing. We need foreign correspondents who have special qualifications for the areas they are to report, who have studied these areas and are competent in the language of the people whose activity they are to report. Theodore White, one of our distinguished correspondents, says "A fast pencil and a good pair of legs aren't enough for a foreign correspondent." Some editors need to learn that. On the strategic news desks that handle the cabled dispatches to prepare them for the newspaper, we need educated men who understand the information they are handling. They need time to consider it, to look up references in the well-stocked library that every newspaper should have and few do have, to write in background if it is needed. They need authority to hold back a report if it looks doubtful, confused or inadequate, until they can get a story that makes sense to them and informs the reader. They need to be free of the insensate time pressure to rush into type the latest bulletin even if it adds nothing but confusion to what they had earlier. *The Christian Science Monitor* will wait a day if necessary to make sure that its story means something. Or they will come in several days later with full background treatment, when most papers have forgotten the subject in the rush to the latest sensation. Continuity is one of the greatest needs of the reader on important issues, and especially if they are remote and unfamiliar to him. Continuity on anything is one of the most serious lacks in most newspapers. You'd think they were in business only today, or anticipated a wholly new set of readers each day to whom they owe no responsibility for what they got them excited about yesterday. Readers need to know how the story came out; what happened after yesterday's banner headline. If the newspaper is the poor man's university, as it claims to be, it needs to take a leaf from the universities, to staff with trained people and give them time to read and study and authority to exercise trained judgment in the interest of an informed report for the reader. We are a long way short of that kind of service of information, and the crises of our times increasingly demand it.

It costs nothing (except perhaps a bit of sensationalism) to make the headlines agree with the text of the story—especially not make headlines state an event as fact, but in the body of the piece hint that it is rumor.

Foreign news often is not read because: (a) it is not well written; (b) the strange names and what has gone on before are unknown to the reader. The papers should provide a box giving a synopsis of pertinent information.

An effort should be made to reduce the practice of ascribing stories to unknown people such as "Diplomatic sources say," and "According to high Washington officials," to a minimum. Protecting an important news source is understandable. But this dodge is being used as a cover for half the unconfirmed rumors floating around bars and restaurants. The reader deserves better treatment than this.

Last, reporters should be paid more than the mechanics in the back room. The editorial part of a paper (or TV station or radio station) is what makes it good or bad. Today reporters frequently not only are paid less than linotype operators, but they have more pressure on them. They must have an incentive, and time to read and think.

If a correspondent goes on a free junket (when commercial airlines or steamers are available) provided by the U. S. Government, a foreign government, or a private commercial organization, we, the readers, deserve to know that someone with publicity in mind is paying for the trip. There should be a boxed notice such as: "Japan Air Lines paid our reporter's expenses for a thirty-day tour to Japan. Equivalent value of tickets, housing, and meals is $3600." If the writer has his expenses paid by a foreign government, the reporter is acting as a foreign agent—even if his article is entirely factual. I suggest that editors study the Department of Justice's ruling for this. (Incidentally, there was one journalist who wrote several flattering books on President Rhee. Readers had no way of knowing that the author was being paid by Rhee.)

Suggesting steps to improve the press coverage of foreign affairs is an almost impossible assignment because publishing a good newspaper in this hectic age is a most difficult job. There is little doubt that the average reporter is a dedicated man who will risk his life to get a story. But where international news is concerned, the story must travel a long and tenuous path between point of origin and publication at home. First, the reporter must find the news and then dig out the facts from an alien environment. Next, the story must be cabled to America, sometimes from a place where there are few communications facilities and where it is subject to local censorship.

Upon arriving in the United States the story is analyzed by the editors for value and perspective. An immediate decision must be made as to which geographic areas in America might have an interest in it (I am speaking of the wire services which supply eighty per cent of our foreign news). The story is then retransmitted to area headquarters, which reanalyzes the story before putting it on the wires to individual papers. When it arrives at the local paper a third evaluation process takes place. Should it go on page one or be buried on page twelve? When this has been decided then a headline—limited to a specified number of letters—must be supplied in a matter of minutes. Everything is done in a mad rush because late news is considered no news.

Even though the editor and reporters may wish to fill the paper with important national and international news, there usually are two inhibiting presences hovering over them: the publisher and the business manager. The paper must make money or there will be no paper at all. In the opinion of most newspaper executives, the only way to avoid bankruptcy is to give the customers what they want.

The customers apparently don't want foreign news. They generally buy a paper to read of local scandals, comic strips, society news, advice to the lovelorn, horoscopes, sports, and other entertainment features.

The press is dependent on the two wire services for foreign news. These gauge their coverage to the average demands of their client papers. What is needed is a higher level of demand, more informed and more critical, to provide more adequate foreign reporting to match our global responsibilities.

With the exception of a small number of rich, well-established papers, magazines, and broadcasting systems, publishers cannot afford their own adequate foreign-news staffs.

There are a few suggestions above on how the press can improve its product, but part of the problem rests with the customers. If the average citizen is not interested in more than a mediocre press on international matters, then a mediocre press is what he will continue to get. If he clamors long and hard enough for a wider and more significant news coverage, then the chances are good he will get something better.

If your newspaper, television station, or magazine is inadequate (and the chances are that it is), then you share a large percentage of the guilt. Only if you express a demand for a more informed and informing American journalism will those who own the presses be seriously moved to provide it.

11

Specifics at a
Personal Level

(Pertaining to the duties and powers of the man and woman in the street—from the clubwoman to the plumber, from the father of teen-agers to the stenographer—from the citizen to his government)

WHAT has gone before concerns action by organized forces such as the government, universities, churches, and the press, already involved in national affairs. What follows concerns the unorganized force which stems from the average man or woman who wants to participate, at least in a small, intelligent way, in the control of his nation's fate, but who holds back his opinions because he feels he has not the training or influence to speak effectively.

The average man or woman can have a powerful effect on the national scene once the realization strikes home that no voice goes unnoticed, particularly if it is raised in intelligent question, objection, or praise. The unorganized civilian is potentially the greatest force of all. There is a politician's maxim that election victories are scored by those who realize that votes are counted one-by-one-by-one-by-one.

Naturally it is easier to marshal the one-by-one-by-one if a coordinated effort is applied. Perhaps the greatest untapped potential in the field of public affairs are the women's clubs of America. There are those who have told me that it is hopeless to try to interest women's clubs in activities outside the local community, but I cannot believe this to be so. The world has become local, and clubs whose services have been so unstinting and effective in projects such as Red Cross, safety drives, and civic beauty, need only to be convinced that their enthusiasm is urgently needed in the struggle for national survival.

If the pressure and common sense of millions of clubwomen is applied to the problem of keeping the nation informed, nothing could resist them. Not only will citizens become more knowledgeable, but also our elected officials and governmental agencies will be forced to become expert in the fulfilling of their difficult duties.

Because I suspect that women's clubs have a keen interest in this national requirement (I have received many forceful, penetrating letters from them), I suggest that in each organization, committees for informing the nation on foreign affairs be formed. Have the committees write to Congressmen and Senators, requesting them to supply short, monthly reports on specific countries—say, for example, Thailand in March, France in April, Laos in May, the Congo in June, etc. Committees should ask the Congressmen to answer questions such as the following:

1. Has Communism been active in —— (name of country) in the last two years? How?

2. Has Communist influence increased in —— in the last year?

3. What is the reason for the increase?

4. Has Communist trade increased in —— in the last few years? (Be sure to ask this question for Afghanistan.) Why? Has U. S. trade there increased or decreased?

5. How many Americans are officially stationed in ——, including all members of Embassy, ICA, USIS, and the military? How many dependents are residing there?

6. How many read, write, and speak the language of the country?

7. Why such a small number (if it is less than 60%)?

8. What is being done to properly train our people for serving abroad in the way of language, customs, culture, religion, etc.? If there is a school, how many have attended it and for how long? What is the curriculum?

9. How many are attending school while living in ——, and for how many hours a week?

10. How many foreigners are employed by the United States in ——? Give a breakdown of their positions.

11. How much does it cost to support one American in ——? This should include all the funds required to maintain him. It should include transportation to and from the overseas port, the cost of maintaining the PX and the commissary, the cost of transporting the supplies to the commissary and PX from America, pay, extra "hardship allowance," housing allowance, cost of supplying him with official local transportation (such as car, etc.). It should

include the total cost of government-supplied movies and other entertainment, the expense of rest camps in the area, and cost of maintaining medical facilities and doctors. Add all of these and divide by the number of people and the average cost will be determined. George V. Allen, ex-director of USIS, said the cost to maintain one American overseas is about $20,000 a year. My estimate, for Asia, is about $28,000 a year. We as citizens deserve to know exactly how much it is for each country.

12. What is the total amount of money spent in each foreign nation per year by the United States? This should include foreign aid, military aid, grants, education, and cost of maintaining our people. You may get a reply from your Congressman saying this information is classified. If so, raise the roof. The Communists know what our activities are all over the world. Why shouldn't we know too?

The questions above are suggestions. Each club's Committee for Informing the Nation on Foreign Affairs undoubtedly will have many questions of its own.

The Committee for Informing the Nation on Foreign Affairs might suggest to your Congressmen and Senators that other citizens might like to have the same information. Therefore, perhaps, they should mail the replies to your questions to every newspaper in their districts.

I am certain that local newspapers will be proud to publish the Congressmen's replies—not only because they contain important information but also because your local organization, as an active and patriotic group, has stimulated the flow of news.

I assure you that if ten women's clubs in each state insist on answers to specific questions on a different foreign country every month—Congress will pay attention and become increasingly knowledgeable in foreign affairs.

Another program which some women's clubs have carried out successfully is the bringing of foreign students to the United States. If an organization embarks on this project it should make it clear that the foreign student need not speak English; and that the grant will include a period of English study. A foreign high-school student would be effective, because he or she can attend school in your home town, no matter where it is, and could easily board with a local family at little expense once the student has arrived. Remember that rich, English-speaking foreign families can provide for their own children's education in America. Bring over a poor child; and if he is from Asia or Africa, don't forget that about 90% of the population is rural. The Asians and Africans want to learn modern farming, practical mechanics, and so on.

Clubs will find that the local newspapers and colleges are glad to help groups willing to learn about foreign affairs. If requested, most editors and college presidents will send a representative to your meetings to give a brief rundown on world events. And also answer questions (such as, perhaps, why is there so little foreign news in the paper?). At any rate, get news experts to your meetings for a fifteen-minute foreign news roundup.

Finally, then, clubwomen should urge other women's organizations in the community to form an Area Committee for Informing the Nation on Foreign Affairs. Women organized can change the nation.

Clubs aside, women as individuals may be the most quietly influential people in the United States. Imperceptibly they mold the tone of the family, the community and the nation.

Any interest which housewives take in public affairs is reflected and multiplied by their children, their husbands, and their friends. One mother I know, for example, suggested to her twelve-year-old daughter that she adopt a Korean orphan as a correspondence "brother." The adoption (via mail) cost fifteen dollars a month. Naturally this was too expensive an undertaking for the twelve-year-old to do alone. The mother asked if perhaps her classmates at school wouldn't like to join in the project.

The classmates were delighted; and each contributed fifty cents a month to the orphan's upkeep. But, of course, the thirty girls *didn't want to adopt a child from a land about which they knew nothing.* Because their new "brother" lived in Korea, they had to find out something about its history and customs. They began studying what people in Korea eat, what kind of clothes they wear, what the major occupations are, the customs and traditions. What are the summers like? The winters? What about the songs and the dances?

In this manner the mother stimulated thirty American children into learning about a foreign land; and indirectly involved them in U. S. foreign policy.

I know another mother who, when she hears that foreign

children are in town, asks them home for the day or weekend. Her own youngsters, as a result, now are corresponding with a dozen children all over the world. They are saving money—earned by mowing lawns, baby-sitting, and washing cars—in order to go overseas in a few years and visit these people. In the meantime, without effort, they are acquiring an interest in events happening abroad. Faraway places no longer are just strange-sounding names to them. They are, instead, the homes of their friends; and they read the newspaper accounts of events there with concern.

On an airplane last month I met an eighteen-year-old American girl on her way to India. It was her mother who had made the trip possible. Knowing that most of the 40,-000 foreign students in the United States are lonely, her mother made a practice of inviting Indian students to their home over the holidays. She had got the names by writing the dean of a college three hundred miles away. Over a ten-year period this family had been host to thirty Indian students. Now the Indians had reciprocated by inviting the American teen-ager to visit their country—with a round-trip ticket included.

Still another mother had encouraged her children to write to "pen pals" overseas. I learned about this when, at Cambridge, I heard a most illuminating discussion on the Japanese riots by a young lady at Radcliffe. When I enquired the source of her information, she said, "For the last four years I've been corresponding with a student in Japan. She was in the riots and wrote me about what happened."

There is no end to what housewives can do to get their families knowledgeable and interested in foreign affairs.

Still in the home, the influence exerted by the father is another source of lasting good in the training of those who will build the future. It usually is the man-of-the-house who orders a year's subscription to *The New York Times, The Christian Science Monitor,* or *The Economist.* And if he reads good papers and magazines (and watches informative television shows), the rest of the family usually does likewise.

I know one household where the father asks questions almost every evening at dinner about that day's news. "What important thing happened in Germany yesterday?" "What is the significance of the revolt which took place in such-and-such-a-land?" "What are the names—and how do you pronounce them—of the three major leaders in Thailand?"

At first no one except the father knew the answers. But after a week the youngsters (teen-agers) began to fight over who should see the paper first; and then *they* began asking questions of their own.

If you try this in your home, don't underestimate your children. They will soon become first-class news analysts. It will not be too long before knowledge of events is simple stuff; and they will want to tackle tough questions. Here are a few father can throw at them:

1. Do the headlines agree with the story?

2. Is the newspaper reporter an eye-witness to the event? If not, who is the source of the information?

3. When the President makes a speech, does the news-

paper's account coincide with the actual speech? (Note: *The New York Times* has verbatim transcripts of the President's talks and news conferences.)

4. Is the United States carrying out a sensible foreign policy in such-and-such country? If not, what should we do? (Note for parents: the original thinking of your children on these matters may surprise you.)

Although this family game is aimed primarily at the youngsters (12–20), the effect on father will be almost miraculous. Whether he likes it or not he will become an expert on international events. Pride will make him try to stay ahead of his youngsters. As a result the members of his car pool, his office, and his club will find themselves dragged into the same line of conversation.

Another father I know takes his sixteen-year-old son to evening meetings whenever a foreigner is scheduled to speak. But first he asks his son to read something about the foreigner's country—even if it is only the account in the encyclopedia. Several times I have heard adults say, "You know, that boy asks more intelligent questions than we do." Sadly enough, they are right.

Another area in which the average man and woman can exert a powerful influence in educating America for its role in the world is that of the school system. Through teachers, P.T.A.'s, school boards, and by persuasion and example, schools can be persuaded to expand their world affairs programs.

In my experience, teen-agers seem to pick up an interest in world affairs quickly if given a sensible chance. Starting with junior year in high school, it seems to me that there should be a current-events class which offers a general scheme of work something like the following:

Each student would be assigned a foreign country as *his*. One student may have Poland, another Cambodia, another Sweden, and so on. The first task is to read about the nation and give the rest of the class a short talk on where the country is, its population, major industries, history in brief, and present problems.

The next task is to make a scrapbook on the country. Perhaps the most efficient way is to have the class subscribe to a couple of copies of *The New York Times* and clip it every day, each student getting the columns on the nation which is his. Once a month (or whatever interval is most convenient for the teacher) the young expert gives the class a brief account of what is happening in *his* country.

Such a project has met with great success in the Punahou School in Honolulu. The few conversations I have had with the student "specialists" were exhilarating. The teen-agers knew their facts far better than the large majority of adults; and they exhibited rare enthusiasm for world affairs which came from the excitement of having informed themselves instead of having had information thrust upon them—from having thought for themselves rather than having memorized pre-thought ideas.

At Punahou the "foreign experts" have developed an awareness of other nations' needs—and their political significance. One lad said, "The million Koreans being repatriated from Japan are choosing Communist North Korea over South Korea. The major reason is that there is housing in the North and hardly any in the South . . ."

Another student interrupted, "I read where someone has invented a machine which makes bricks out of anything—straw, wood, vegetable pulp—mixed with earth. Anyone can operate it. This machine turns out bricks any place under any conditions—faster and cheaper than all present methods . . .

"Why don't we make this one of our national Peace Corps Projects?"

The students have written to obtain all information on the brick machine. Soon you may see youngsters from Hawaii building houses in South Korea during their vacations. This chain of events started because a few teen-agers were familiar with foreign affairs.

Finally, the basic truth of personal action in public affairs is that no voice goes unheard. For example:

Several years ago Paul Hoffman was up for confirmation as a government official. A conservative northern Senator, a long-time friend of Hoffman, was implacably opposed to the appointment.

Hoffman called on him. Their conversation went along these lines.

"Senator," said Hoffman, "I hear that . . ."

"Paul, I simply can't support your appointment. The ground swell of public opinion is violently against you."

"A ground swell? What do you mean?"

The senator pushed a buzzer and a secretary entered.

"Get me the folder on Paul Hoffman."

A few moments later she brought in a filing envelope

and gave it to the Senator. With a grand gesture, he dumped the contents on the desk. There were *six* letters opposing the appointment of Paul Hoffman.

The lesson is this: In a democracy where so many are inarticulate, the voices that do speak carry enormous weight. It is possible that five or six thousand aroused, dedicated, and objective, well-informed Americans could, just by putting their opinions forthrightly and honestly, effect the kind of blueprint for success suggested in this book.

Whenever you object to something; whenever you have a constructive way to improve matters; whenever you want to know the facts of an issue—write, call, or telegraph. Write the President, your Congressman, Senator, newspaper, your radio and TV station. If you don't get satisfaction, then follow it up with more letters, calls and telegrams.

When election time comes, examine and evaluate the candidates' past records. Don't accept their word for anything. If the candidate is up for re-election, look up and see exactly how he voted on all issues. *The New York Times* usually carries this information on major pieces of policy or legislation. By writing to The Government Printing Office, Washington 25, D.C., you can get the biggest publishing bargain in the world. For a nominal fee you can get reports on all Congressional matters concerning foreign affairs. It's a lot of printed matter, but it contains exactly what your Congressman or Senator had to say about foreign relations. At the very least, urge your newspaper and library to subscribe.

At local levels we can ask challenging questions at political meetings. When this kind of interest occurs across the nation—and it is effective even when small numbers take action—the candidates will be forced to know their business.

Subscribe to a good newspaper. In my opinion there are only a handful of first-class newspapers in the United States as far as national and international affairs are concerned. They include:

The New York Times
The New York Herald Tribune
The Washington Post
The Washington Star
The Christian Science Monitor
The Wall Street Journal (for foreign news)
The Chicago Daily News
The Chicago Tribune
The Louisville Courier Journal
The Baltimore Sun
The Minneapolis Tribune
The Milwaukee Journal

There may be others, and some editors may disagree; but I don't think there will be many objections. Of one thing we can be certain, on foreign news *The New York Times* is the most complete paper in the world. The best judge on this delicate matter is yourself. I suggest you take a month's subscription to any good paper and compare it with the one in your home town.

IV
A Response to
Challenge

12

A Response to Challenge

AFTER *A Nation of Sheep* was drafted, the author, in addressing a West Coast audience, gave what amounted to a preview of its contents. At the end of the address, the discussion was opened to the floor. Numerous questions were discussed, and what follows is a digest of the most revealing and frequently asked:

Question: If we write letters, send telegrams, and raise hell the way you suggested, won't we be branded as cranks, eccentrics, or maybe even as Communists?

Answer: You probably will.

But Jefferson was considered a radical, and Lincoln an extremist. People thought William Allen White to be bad-mannered when he started his vigorous *Emporia Gazette*. Edison and Fulton both were sneered at as being nuts. The list is endless.

Your question boils down to: Do you prefer being an American individualist (eccentric or crank, in your words) —with all the hazards involved; or do you prefer to be a citizen of a spineless nation which—eventually—may have a Khrushchev as president. Do you favor a bungling do-nothing, know-nothing America—simply because you and a million others are afraid to speak up?

That's the big decision you have to make.

Question: If we write letters to newspapers or our Congressmen or the State Department—even the President—we'll probably get a whitewash in reply. How do we know they're telling the truth? How can we check on it? How do we know they'll even see our letters?

Answer: It's possible that you may receive a whitewash reply—especially if it concerns blunders or failures which the bureaucrats aren't too happy about.

But the democratic process is a strange animal. Its efficiency is in direct proportion to the percentage of citizens who show interest in government. For example, if one hundred people from your district wrote your Congressman about Laos—the Congressman (probably knowing little about Laos) would send the queries to the Department of State, ICA, and the Department of Defense; and request that these agencies supply the necessary information.

Several things would result.

(1) Gradually the government would realize that there is public interest in the subject (including a Congressman on whom the agencies are dependent for future appropri-

ations). If the same kind of questions poured in from ten Congressmen, the Department of State, ICA, and the Department of Defense would be very careful in their replies. Officials are well aware that Congress has the authority to send observers to Laos to see things first hand—and also to hold investigations.

Furthermore, the Congressman who receives your queries depends on you for his re-election. If enough citizens ask specific questions on foreign affairs, he must, for his own political survival, learn something about the subject and make sure that you do not get a run-around.

Also, if hundreds of questions are sent in, the press will get wind of the matter. This is news; and the newspapers have no choice but to dig into the subject themselves.

In a free country, the interest shown by individuals in governmental affairs tends to snowball. The election principle of "one by one by one by one" is the way of winning. Your one letter, telephone call, or telegram may well be the factor which stops a bad appointment, initiates a sound law, or causes a high official to change a foreign-policy decision.

This is the law of functioning democracies. A nation operates honestly and well as long as citizens show interest. But when citizens become apathetic, then dictatorship, ignorance, and national decline take over.

When you make excuses such as, "Why try, I'll get a white-wash job anyway?" or "I don't want to take a chance of being labeled as an eccentric or pinko," or "I don't know whom to write," or "Why not leave the problems to the experts, that's why we have them in government?"—

then you are too lazy and apathetic to deserve a democratic way of life. What's more, you won't have it much longer.

Question: There's nothing new about the frauds and corruptions in Laos, Korea, and China. We heard about them a long time ago. Why have them in this book?

Answer: You have touched the nerve center of *A Nation of Sheep.* Certainly you heard about our international blunders a long time ago. But you only learned about them after the failures no longer could be hidden. I will answer your question by asking you two questions:

(1) Why did neither you nor the government or the press have knowledge of the corruptions and blunders during the many years they were developing?

(2) After you heard about the bungling and inefficiencies, what action did you take personally? You didn't do a thing. You shook your head and turned to the sports page, the comics, or the society columns.

The great mistakes in Korea, Laos, and China are repeated in this book to remind you that you did not know about them until late in the game, and then you neither grasped their significance nor did anything to correct them. You exhibited no indignation, no citizen's interest. You passively kept chewing your cud, feeling secure in a nation of sheep. And while you silently accepted disgraceful performances, a handful of Communists have gained influence over half the world.

Question: I admit that most of us are poor citizens; and that it is up to us to remedy the situation. But isn't there some way that the Congress or the President could prime the pump—you know, make it fashionable to participate in government, to stand up and be counted, to give our opinions on public issues?

Answer: President Ramon Magsaysay of the Philippines had the same problem. The only voices he could hear were those of the politicians in Manila and a few biased newspapers. He wanted to know what the people were thinking. To accomplish this he did a remarkable thing. He made it possible for any Filipino to send a telegram to the President for only ten centavos.

The system was a success. Filipinos found it easy and cheap to communicate directly with the President. They knew that he did not read every telegram personally, but that a special presidential committee (and no one else) saw the messages, and the committee briefed the chief executive.

Perhaps we, too, could have an arrangement by which a citizen anywhere in USA could telegraph his Congressman, Senator, or the President for a moderate sum, perhaps twenty-five cents.

True, we could say more in a letter, but most of us somehow don't seem to be able to break through the "time and laziness" barrier; and the letters seldom get written. But if we could send a telegram for a quarter, it would be simple. One could phone the telegraph office and say, "I want to send a message to the President, and here is what I want to say . . ."

The twenty-five-cent charge would automatically be added to your telephone bill.

· 185 ·

Question: I am skeptical about your statements that the *N. Y. Times* is so much better than our local papers for foreign news. Can you clarify this, please?

Answer: What newspapers have we available here? Please gather them up and count the columns of foreign news in each.

Note: Here is the results of the count for the newspapers available for January 10, 1961:

Los Angeles Herald Express—4 columns of foreign news.

Oakland Tribune—5 columns.

San Francisco Chronicle—5 columns.

N. Y. Times—68 columns.

Question: Do you think the blunders and lies and lack of information should be blamed on the Eisenhower Administration?

Answer: No. Although the Eisenhower administration was not vigorous in giving us a realistic picture of national events, an uninformed public can only blame itself. Ignorance and lack of interest on the part of citizens has become a national characteristic regardless of administrations. Our political curiosity and boldness has atrophied, perhaps from generations of overconfidence caused by the easy security of geographical protection and natural prosperity.

If the President himself makes an effort to be intimate with national and world events—and exhibits this tendency in his public statements and press conferences—it will become contagious. It will become just as fashionable to know what is happening in Ghana or Poland or Laos as it is to be able to quote a batting average or repeat the latest gossip on a movie star. Mr. Kennedy's opportunities for revitalizing the nation in this respect are limitless.

Question: Then you mean for your book to be a guide and a blueprint for the future . . . and use the past only as a teacher?

Answer: That is correct.

V
Conclusion

13
Conclusion

THE preface of this book pointed out that in response to *The Ugly American,* we received over 8,000 querying letters. They came from every corner of our country and from all kinds of people. In one form or another they asked the same desperate questions:

What can the average American do about the frightful posture of the United States in foreign affairs?

How can the man in the street and the woman in the kitchen help prevent the blunders by which we are aiding our enemies all over the world?

Over and over, in the mail, at lectures, in public conveyances, in homes, over the telephone, people incessantly have repeated, "What can I do to help?"

Obviously they would not have asked these questions had they known what was going on nationally and internationally. If they had knowledge, the answers would have been obvious.

Likewise our officials would not be blundering all over the place if they possessed the facts of world affairs.

America has more assets than any other nation in the

globe. We have more material wealth, more educational facilities, more freedom. If we fail it is only because we are stupid and permit aggressive nations to take advantage of our mistakes.

This is no miraculous revelation. All of us instinctively sense that foolish errors are the cause of our failures. However, few people angrily *demand* that action be taken to correct matters. And fewer yet recommend how. Instead they wring their hands pitiably and bleat, "What can I do? What can I do? All is lost."

We are acting like a nation of sheep—not a vigorous community of bold, well-informed Americans.

This book has briefly tried to accomplish three things:

1. Analyze the basic causes of our debilitating national ignorance, both official and unofficial.

2. Make clear that officials are direct reflections of you and me. If we are ignorant and apathetic, then our government also is ignorant and apathetic.

3. Offer a few specific suggestions of how ordinary citizens can, in their everyday lives, become better informed; and some possible methods for making our amateur officials into effective professionals.

The final and vital point of this book is that the state of the nation depends upon individual citizens. It is we who, in a democracy, must set the examples for our officials.

Some sociologists and political scientists have told me that I am wrong. They say that the well-being of a nation never can originate from the people. It comes only from the efforts of a strong leader.

I disagree.

I believe that only if we, you and I, inform ourselves and then act with energy and courage according to our knowledge, only then will we breed strong leaders, principled and informed. They come from us; they are among us in potential. We must create a climate in which they will flourish.

Every moment reveals a new frontier studded with challenges. To survive, we must stop acting like a nation of sheep; instead we must once again become patriotic revolutionaries. We must move and grow with changing events. So long as we recognize and understand the forces and facts of our world we can win. We must drive ourselves to stay well informed; we must not be afraid to move ahead and change at a bold, vigorous pace. The nation which stands still, apathetically hoping that everything soon will be all right, has surrendered its chance of survival. An accelerating history will roll over it.

You whose eyes scan these lines and whose hands hold this book inherit the heart and stamina to sustain our nation in its hour of need. But you do not have the luxury of waiting until an obviously glorious and heroic moment arrives—that moment when you have the opportunity of performing well with flags waving and bands playing. Every moment is potentially glorious and heroic. A citizen must perform a citizen's duties in everyday life. There is no armistice; there is no vacation from the present war.

Now—as you read the last page—you can reach for your

writing materials, for your newspaper, for the telephone—and take the first step of personal action. The results will come and they will be visible. I suggest that you hurry. The television screens may be bright and our comfortable homes may be warm; but outside it is beginning to grow dark and cold.